Front cover image by Kristin Schuchman
Interior book design concept by Cassi Ott
Edited by Kristin Thiel
Proofed by Alexa Hopson and Erin Frank
Illustrations by SpiffyJ/iStockPhoto.com
Special thanks to Julianne Chatelaine for offering invaluable developmental editorial consulting.

978-1-7353512-0-9 (ebk.)   978-1-7353512-1-6 (pbk.)

Printed by A Mighty Flame Publishing in the United States of America.

First printing edition 2020.

A Mighty Flame Publishing, 624 SE 70th Avenue, Portland, OR 97215
www.sparkacareer.com

The DIY WEBSITE WORKBOOK

7 steps for building a website that engages and converts

a simple, step-by-step
guide for creating
a compelling
web presence

Kristin Schuchman

Contents

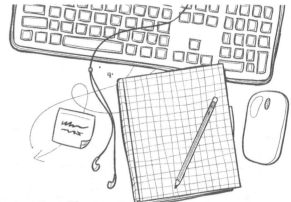

Introduction

Whether you want to build or revamp your own website or outsource your web development, this workbook is for you. Most solopreneurs plunge headlong into the abyss of building a site without taking the time to deeply consider what their website should accomplish, who it should reach, and why it exists.

I'm assuming you picked up this workbook because you want to do the smart thing – plan your website more strategically to ensure more success. You understand how vital a web presence is to run a business. Websites are often the first introduction a client has to a business—a chance to make a first impression and, if designed to effectively speak to its intended audience, able to convert viewers into paying clients. I'm also guessing that the prospect of a workbook was enticing because it suggests that I will break down the process into easy, bite-size pieces, not leave you to venture down a technical rabbit hole that will leave you disillusioned and frustrated.

You're right. The websites I've built on behalf of clients, including myself, have actually been fun to create and, at their best, are an authentic expression of the brand and person they represent. And I designed this workbook to be something you can work through quickly if you're under a deadline or linger and spend time with if you're still several weeks away from launching your website. (I recommend you take at least a day for each chapter.) This workbook is structured as 7 Steps of Building a Website:

Step 1: Preplanning Your Website
Step 2: Understanding Your Audience
Step 3: Converting Viewers into Clients
Step 4: Building Your Website Architecture
Step 5: Creating Dynamic Content
Step 6: Getting Your Website Built
Step 7: Care and Feeding (AKA Maintenance)

Since the best websites are intuitive yet logical, I've designed this workbook to stimulate both your best left- and right-brained thinking. Tap into both sides of your brain as much as you can and invite colleagues who understand your brand to collaborate when you're stuck.

I like metaphors, as you'll soon notice, so I want you to start thinking of your website as a physical boutique (even if you have a service-focused business). Some people will see your site for a second and, like a hurried pedestrian, walk on by. Others will linger and make a note to return but not come into your store in that moment (that is, click on more links that take them further into your website). Still others will enter and spend some time but, despite being duly impressed, not make a purchase right away. Some will enter, love what they see, and push "Purchase" or "Book a Session" on their first visit.

You want to be thinking about how you serve all of these customers—even the lookie-loos, who may come back when they really need you or your product—as you plan your website. As you would with a physical store, make it a place people want to spend time, that adds value to their day and leaves them with the unique impression of yourself and your brand that only you can deliver.

When you're ready to build this "store" or hire a web developer to do so (**Step 6: Getting Your Website Built**) advises you on pros and cons for each), I am confident that the exercises you complete in this workbook will provide a solid foundation for the process.

At a minimum, I emphasize the importance of staying in control of your website. Even if you hire a web developer, make sure that you have complete control over your domain registration, hosting, and any "dashboard" used to update your website. This is non-negotiable. Any developer who will not provide you with control of these things should be dismissed immediately. I've heard too many stories of business owners losing access to websites because they didn't secure control of these features. If you take nothing else from this workbook, please heed my advice on that caveat.

Someone said once, "Man plans, and God laughs." I like to say, "Business owner doesn't plan her website, and the gods of the internet snicker quietly as she toils away at her website and then doesn't understand why it doesn't attract clients." It's not as catchy, but I think it makes its point.

So, roll up your sleeves and start planning your site—try to finish the entire workbook before you begin building, but give yourself permission to stay somewhat fluid and flexible. Think of this process as reviewing the ingredients list of a recipe. (Told you I dig imagery.) As you work through this workbook, you will get a chance to combine the key ingredients to create a killer website. For now, you are just reading it, making a few notes, and bookmarking sections for future reference. Okay, let's get going.

Step One
Pre-Planning Your Website

Housekeeping

Keeping Your Website Secure

As I mentioned in the introduction, I like everyone to think of their website as a brick-and-mortar building, not only in the way it represents their business but in the sense that it will be built methodically brick by brick and structured to last. It doesn't matter if you're not selling products—the metaphor still applies. You're "hanging your shingle" on your website as you would above your actual storefront.

Just as you would take care in distributing the keys to your store, you need to be discreet about whom you entrust with access to your website. If you absorb nothing else in this book, please write this down:

Keep control of your website domain and your host.

Pretend I'm Hans and Franz from SNL and imagine me pointing my finger at you and saying, "Hear me now and believe me later!" This is seriously important:

Keep control of your website domain and your host.

You may be asking yourself, "What the *(!#%& is a **domain** and what the ^$@(!% is a **host**?"

Many people think the domain and the host are the same—it's important that you understand the distinction. Your **domain** is the website address or URL you assign to your website, like www.ilovefunsocks.com. The **host** is the place that owns the server where your website resides. Companies like Bluehost and StartLogic offer hosting services, and most hosting services let you register your domain name through their service. I recommend you find a service that offers both so that when you or your website builder are creating your site, it's easier to set up since you're only dealing with one company.

If you think of your website as a boutique, your domain is like the actual address at which your site resides while the host is sort of like your landlord. They let you reside in the space, but you have to pay them rent. Your website host provides a plan that give you a certain amount of **bandwidth** (or room for storage), and most starter plans offer "unlimited bandwidth," which is ample for most solopreneur ventures. If you do ever want to expand your bandwidth, however, you'll want to change your plan with your host, just like you'd discuss with your landlord your plans to knock down the wall to enlarge your boutique's floor space.

This metaphor isn't perfect since you can always transfer your domain to another host. It's very important that you are named as the registrar of your domain at all times. It is tempting to check out on this piece, but I urge you not to. I've heard too many horror stories about businesses who let a website professional or a "friend" register their domain only to find out months later that they needed to change their host, and the website professional or friend was MIA or unresponsive. Technically, whoever registers a domain owns it, so if you want to own your website, don't let this detail slide.

Your **email address** is tied up with domain and host too. Think of your email address as the mailbox where you pick up your mail. For most businesses, it includes the domain name (kristin@ ilovefunsocks.com), and the backup files for it are stored on the host. Even when using online email platforms like Gmail, your host will store a backup copy of all emails. (You also want to retain tight control of your host, since anyone with full access to your host can read backup copies of your emails.)

For all matters of your website, make sure you have secure passwords for the host, the domain registration, and all email addresses. Keep them in a secure location and only share them with your most trusted employees and colleagues. Don't pay a website developer until she has provided these passwords. In the appendix, I have a glossary of technical website terms, like "DNS servers" and "IP addresses," but that's as technical as I'm going to get for now.

Following is a place to record the contact information for your web developer (if you plan to use one) as well as the services you choose to host your website and register your domain.

Name of Web Developer:
Phone Number:
Email Address:
Website Address:
Best Way to Contact:

Domain Registrar:
Hosting Service:

Choosing a Domain Name

If you haven't already registered your domain name, let me provide a few quick tips.

Tip 1: Keep your domain name short and sweet. Try to keep it to five syllables or fewer (not including the "dot" and "com").

Tip 2: Say it out loud to several people and make sure they understand what you're saying. The English language has a multitude of words that sound alike, so make sure when you say something like "for friends dot com," people aren't hearing "four friends dot com." Also stay away from words that are hard to spell or too obscure. You can get away with this if you are super-niched and you know your audience will appreciate it, but you have to make a case for using a URL. Hard-core fans of Johann Wolfgang von Goethe may love "Giddy for Goethe" but most people will hear, "Giddy for Gerta." If you think your potential audience is going to seek you out nevertheless, by all means, use the URL. (I would seek out the website www.giddyforgoethe.com, so there may be enough of us nerds to make it a hit.)

Tip 3: Pay attention to how it looks when written out.
BeAtEase.com may seem like a great domain name for a business but has the unfortunate tendency to look like BeATease or BeatEase when written out in all-lowercase letters: www.beatease.com

Tip 4: Make it memorable.
A friend told me several years ago that a graphic designer friend of hers used the domain www.ihatecilantro.com for his portfolio, and I never forgot it, possibly because I too believe this herb to be quite overrated. As of this printing, this bold URL points to a 403 error page, but I never forgot that website address. There's something to be said about names that stay with you years later. Don't be afraid to play with humor, use action words, and appeal to emotion. Like effective branding, a domain can do some heavy lifting as you spread the word about your business.

Tip 5: Don't be afraid to try a new domain extension.
There's never been a better time to reserve a domain now that you are no longer restricted to .com, .net, or .org. Many holistic healers are using the **.health** or **.healthcare** extension, and new domain extensions are released all the time. United Domains (www.uniteddomains.com) does a great job of keeping an updated list of new domain extension releases. These are some examples of new domain extensions that were released in the last few years:

.kids, .ing, .joy, .coach, .accountant, .home, .hotel, .day, .living, .sucks (I dare you to use **.sucks**. It will likely be quite memorable. As of this printing, no one has yet reserved www.cilantro.sucks)

What You Need

The Basics

Trust me—you'll never regret taking the time to plan your website well and lay a solid foundation for a website that will create a dynamic experience for your clients, authentically reflect your brand, and stand the test of time. But there are a few requirements that you would do well to reflect on before you dive in.

At a minimum, you need:
- A basic understanding of how a site works
- A willingness to get somewhat comfortable with data and analytics (or hire someone who is and can tell you about these things clearly and compellingly)
- A clear purpose for your site (drive sales, attract attention for a product or a book or podcast, provide a blogging platform, raise awareness about your business, attract a referral network, etc.)
- The drive to thoughtfully dive into the exercises here and plan your site well from the get-go

Beyond the Basics

Ideally, you'll have:
- A willingness to learn a little HTML
- An understanding of your target market
- The self-awareness to take constructive feedback from others who know more yet the clear-headedness about your company vision to stand firm in your conviction about the best way to represent your brand
- Patience
- A drive to make your website a dynamic, engaging tool to grow your business and not only make it pay for itself but make it something you're incredibly proud to have represent your brand
- A small team "board of directors" you can check in with – a data person, a web designer, a graphic designer, and a writer. If you can find someone with a passion for **SEO**, you'll be cooking with gas. (**SEO** stands for **Search Engine Optimization** and is just a slick way to say that you design your site and write your copy so that people can find your business on Google. More on this in **Step 5: Creating Dynamic Content** and **Step 6: Getting Your Website Built**).

Cost Considerations

Unless you are building a company with a national presence or that needs to have incredibly sophisticated e-commerce and database capabilities, you should be able to build a website for $5,000 to $10,000 at the most. If you are willing to build it yourself on a platform like WordPress, Wix, Weebly, or Squarespace, you can get away with paying less than $500 in setup fees (including hosting and domain subscriptions) and around $9 to $50 per month, depending on the platform.

Depending on your technical acumen, you may or may not possess the desire to update your own website, but I invite you to consider it. Whether you update it once it is constructed or you hire someone else to do so, you should at least know the platform on which it is built so you know whom to hire if your website person quits or completely disappears one day. (It happens.) WordPress, Wix, Squarespace, and Weebly are among the easiest to update. Try to hire a website developer willing to train you on how to update the website. Request this service before she quotes the job. If she isn't willing to do this, find a different developer.

Why Your Website Matters

If you didn't think your website was important, you wouldn't be working through this workbook. I try to keep the planning of a website fun and engaging, yet from the outset, I want you to reflect on why it is worthwhile to take the time to plan your website well.

These are the most common reasons to build a website.

Sell Services, Products, or Both

I'll say it again—your website is not just a brochure. It has the capacity to do so much more. I love Apple products, and I'm an introvert, but when I walk into an Apple store, I want there to be people around me, and I like that there are different products for me to try and play with depending on my mood and ADD level. Your website should be the same way—be willing to respond to an individual's neuro-sensibilities in the moment and lead her where she wants to go.

I want you to think of your website as a place people will experience your business, either for the first time or as an extension of a brand they have interacted with in person. Either way, you will want to do everything a storefront would do: project your values, quality, and personality; invite viewers to spend time and get to know your offerings; convert your viewers to clients; and encourage them to make a mental note or bookmark your site to return to it soon or follow you on social media.

In *Million Dollar Website*, Rebecca Murtagh wrote, "The website is a fluid reflection of your brand within an ever-changing marketplace, the Internet. Just as your offer, service, brand, promotions, and price must continually adapt in order for your organization to maintain its competitive edge, your website must also evolve."

While you may want your website to convert users to customers, you will need to be thoughtful and constantly refine your site to keep it responsive and ensure that it leads users to a **landing page** where people will book a session or buy or download a product. It's called a **landing page** because it's the page you're ultimately leading people to. Think of it as your cash register and make sure the pages that lead users there are fluid, uncluttered, and streamlined. (We'll talk more about this in **Step 4: Building Your Architecture**, in which you will determine how users will navigate the site. Don't worry too much about it for now).

Establish Trust

UX (user experience) design refers to a style of design that deeply considers how a person responds as she interacts with a product or tech tool. UX (sometimes called UI, for "user interface") references **touchpoints**, which are the various ways people will interact with your brand before they are ready to act. These can include visual displays, online ads, word of mouth, print marketing materials—anything that leads people to your business. Your website is arguably the single most powerful touchpoint for your client besides you personally.

Make sure your website does all the things you would do if you were in the room with a visitor:
- Communicates what you stand for with consistency, respect and inclusivity
- Project the emotions and values of your brand (warm and approachable? edgy and irreverent? sunny and high-spirited?)
- Answers all their questions thoroughly and quells their concerns
- Introduces your business with authenticity and a sense of helpfulness
- Gives them a chance to get and keep in touch.

Raise Awareness

When you feel yourself getting overwhelmed, remember that you don't need billions of viewers—you just need the right ones. Among the people you want to reach, be thinking about what you want people to know. As a career counselor, I want stay-at-home moms who want to relaunch to know that most of the barriers to workforce reentry are internal and that most employers are happy to employ people who have taken a break if gaps in employment are explained and candidates are qualified. Think about the things you not only want potential clients to know about you but what you want them to know in general. This will make you stand out and establish your authority and potential to connect with your audience.

1. What are some other reasons you think building a website is worthwhile?

2. What will "sales" look like on your website (product sales, sessions booked, digital downloads, event registrations, etc.)?

3. List some ways your website can engender trust.

4. List some things you really want your clients to know about you. List some things you want your clients to know about your area of expertise. What problems is your business seeking to solve?

5. What do you consider the mission of your website? (Ideally, you can describe your website's mission in 3 minutes or less.)

Research the Competition

Visit 3 websites and go through their sites thoroughly, jotting down notes along the way about what you do and don't like about their sites. Ask yourself, "What would I 'steal,' and how would I make it mine?" and "What would I not do?"

Write down overall aesthetic impressions and how well (or not) the writing and look represent the brand. What can you learn from them?

Ask yourself:

1. Is it hard to find contact information?

2. Is it helping me close the deal (buy products, book an appointment, raise awareness, etc.)? Why or why not?

3. Are clients finding what they are looking for?

4. Is it confusing or hard to use any forms or shopping carts?

5. Am I enticed to stay on the site and spend more time on it?

6. Am I impressed? Why? Am I at all put off? Why?

7. Are any of the links broken?

Step away from this exercise for at least a day after completing it and then ask yourself how you might remedy each problem in one sentence.

If You Have a Website Now...

Go through it as if you were looking at it for the first time, as if you were a potential customer, and write down notes about what you do and don't like about the experience. Do this in a quiet, uninterrupted space.

Ask yourself:

1. Am I proud to have this represent my brand? What would make me prouder?

2. Are any of my links broken? Are there typos? Does anything slow down the load time? (Make a note of these and fix them later. Focus on just experiencing the website right now.)

3. Can people find the specific information (my rates or prices, whether I offer cranial sacral massage, if my bar serves hard cider, etc.) they might be seeking?

Once you've done this with all of your pages, walk away for at least a day. When you return to your notes, sift through them and write down your solution for each "problem" you detected. If you find yourself in a quandary about how you would solve that problem, put a star by it. You'll come back to this section in **Step 4: Building Your Architecture** and make it part of your overall engagement strategy.

If you can't be objective, ask a straight-talking friend or organize a focus group. The goal is to give clients a seamless and engaging experience and encourage them to get on your hook by subscribing, buying, or trying. You want to think about the user and value substance over style. I'm an aesthetic snob, so this is hard for me too, but you lose people online if something takes even a little too long to load or isn't easy to find or fonts don't load properly and look all jumbled. Put the flourishes in but keep things simple.

Try, Buy, or Subscribe

As I mentioned in the Introduction, I like everyone to think of their website as a brick-and-mortar building, not only in the way it represents their business, but in the sense that it will be built methodically brick by brick and structured to last. It doesn't matter if you're not selling products – the metaphor still applies. You're "hanging your shingle" on your website just as you would above your actual storefront.

Too many entrepreneurs think of their website as an online brochure, but these days it has the capacity to do so much more. Not only do I want you to think of it as a 'boutique' that represents your business – I want you to think of it as one that is fully staffed with excellent sales people who can respond to every possible question or concern a client has and invite her to do at least one of three things – **Try, Buy,** or **Subscribe.**

Try

Trying a product or service gives viewers the chance to see what you have to deliver without much commitment. Some examples include:

- Downloadable worksheets, lists of tips, or quizzes in exchange for their email address, which potentially converts them to a subscriber
- Free 15-minute phone call visitors can schedule to see if you are a good fit
- Complimentary or low-priced events (webinars or virtual or in-person meet-and-greets or workshops that viewers can register for to get a taste of your expertise
- Short, free instructional video
- An offer to send a free sample of a product you sell
- A coupon if the viewer shares her email with you (with the understanding she will receive future emails from you)
- A request for a quote of your services

Buy

Buying a product or service on your website converts your viewer into an actual client and marks the beginning of a relationship that you can start to cultivate over time. This can look a few different ways:

- Paid in-person or online consulting, counseling, or coaching sessions or packages
- Registration for a full-priced webinar, e-course, mastermind, or e-book
- Purchase of products to be shipped to the client or tickets for an in-person or online event
- Payment for a subscription to your service or product (or a combination). Blue Apron is arguably a combination of a subscription service for a combined product (the food and recipes) and service (the delivery of food and the website that lets you choose delivery dates and specify meal options).

Subscribe

Subscribing refers to a person keeping in touch with you and is not to be casually dismissed. It may be a lower level of commitment than **Trying** or **Buying**, but it still starts a relationship and displays a certain level of confidence in your business. Viewers show an interest in engaging further with your business by:

- Subscribing to your newsletter
- Following your blog
- Liking or following your business on social media
- Bookmarking your website

Sometimes there may be overlap between Trying and Subscribing, but it's important to distinguish them since the viewer isn't "trying" anything unless she's actively hooked by a coupon or a download. All of these examples can be encouraged by using strategic graphic tools for your site (like buttons and social media icons). We're not going to dive into that now, but I do want you to start thinking about how you would invite viewers to:

1. Try:

2. Buy:

3. Subscribe:

Don't get too detailed yet. Just hold your ideas loosely and put them on the page. You can think through the logistics and specifics in **Step 4: Building Your Architecture**.

Website Prebuild Checklist

Every website is different and should provide users with a unique experience that sets your brand apart and makes an impression. There are, however, basic ingredients that every site should include to offer an optimal user experience. **Simply review this checklist** now, and as you build or revamp your site, refer to it to make sure you can check off all of the boxes. Near the end of the book, on page TK, you'll find a **Website Postbuild Checklist** that you can use to review your site after it's launched.

Use the spaces following each item to make notes as you review the checklist. Again, remember that you're just reviewing this list. Don't get bogged down by the details of how you will accomplish all of these things yet. You're simply absorbing these concepts for now.

Does Your Website...

☐ **Have a Focused Mission?**
Does your website project a clear mission and focus? Is its messaging clear and consistent?

☐ **Convert Viewers Into Clients and/or Followers?**
Is it converting users into customers by leading them to the landing pages? If they are navigating to landing pages, are they purchasing a product, booking an appointment, or signing up for an event or class?

☐ **Invite Active Engagement?**
Does it invite users to return or to try, buy, or subscribe? Does it stimulate their curiosity or inform or surprise them? Does it leave an impression? How do graphics, illustrations, and photos attract interaction? Does it leave them wanting more? Why should they return?

☐ **Offer Clear Navigation and a Fluid User Experience?**
Is its navigation logical and intuitive? Does it offer different brains alternative ways to make their way toward landing pages? Are buttons and links easy to read and understand? Can people easily trace their way back and easily return to pages they may be looking for?

☐ **Offer Easy-To-Find Contact Information?**
Is the contact information easy to find? I like to see contact information on every page.

☐ **Brand You Well?**
Is your website consistent with your brand? Is the branding consistent with the messaging and graphics throughout the site? (We'll talk more about branding in **Step 2: Understanding Your Audience**.)

☐ **Look and Feel Consistent Throughout?**
Does the site feel, sound, and look consistent throughout its pages? Is it written in the same tone and from the same perspective (third person or first person, for example)? Does the imagery look like they are cohesive and harmonious?

☐ **Have a Platform That Is Easy to Update?**
Is your website developer willing to show you how to update your site? Are you willing to learn? If neither of these it true, are you willing to pay someone to update it every time you want to make a change?

☐ **Save You Money by Generating Sales with a Minimum of Effort?**
You're a busy entrepreneur and need to spend your time working on various aspects of your business. Your website takes care and feeding but should not be a complete time suck. It may take time, but if you invest the time it takes in your site navigation and your SEO, your website should generate sales on its own, if you consider that a worthwhile goal.

☐ **Attract Referral Partners?**
Does it attract professionals who will likely refer business to you? Does your website or blog offer information and insight that engages your referral partners?

☐ **Reach Markets You Want to Reach, Not Limiting You to a Geographic Area (If You Have Set Your Sights Beyond Your Local Area)?**
If you are hoping to reach beyond your immediate area, does the website speak to this, or does it limit you geographically? If you are focused on a specific area, does it reflect the culture of that area? How so?

☐ **Stay Under Your Control?**
Are you in complete control of your hosting and domain, including all passwords? Are charges for both under your control? (They should always be; be conscientious about keeping that information current.)

☐ **Feel Expensive to Create or Maintain?**
If you have hired someone else to build it, are you certain there are no hidden expenses? Are they willing to train you on how to update and maintain it, both with content changes and technical updates?

☐ **Appear Easily to the People Who Are Searching for You?**
There's never a better time than when you're building your website to have SEO in mind. Chances are someone out there right now is looking for a business like yours, but she can't find you if your website isn't optimized for the search words she's using. We'll explore this further in **Step 4: Building Your Architecture**.

☐ **Create Excitement In Your Ideal Client When They Find You?**

You should be proud to refer your website to people and feel confident that its content and features are doing everything humanly possible to promote your business. Ideally, it will stir an emotional reaction in your prospective clients and make them feel like they *must* buy your product or service or they *can't wait* to meet you.

☐ **Talk to Your Social Media?**

All of the social media accounts for your business should have icons representing the various platforms on every page of your website (in a static header or footer). Your blog posts should be set up to encourage shares and likes.

☐ **Feature Mixed Media?**

The more media—photography, video, downloadable files—the better. It's not only good for your SEO, it makes you look like you're truly engaged with your business and gives your client more reason to linger and interact. We'll talk about this more in **Step 7: Care and Feeding (AKA Maintenance)**.

☐ **Prize Quality Over Quantity – Attract The "Right" People, Not Just The "Right Number" Of People?**

You may attract millions of viewers with your site, but if they're people who will never buy from you or engage with the site, does it matter? That tree fell in the forest, and no one heard it. Is your target audience finding you, and if so, are they spending time on the website, purchasing, or spreading the word about your site with excitement and vigor?

☐ **Have An Elegant, Easy-To-Use Shopping Cart?**

If your website has e-commerce functionality, is it easy to navigate and understand? Does it offer appropriate options (shipping + handling) and make it clear when users can expect delivery of products or services? Will they see an  automatic confirmation response page after they click "Submit" or "Buy Now" and receive a follow-up email? Do you test this feature regularly?

☐ **Facilitate Optimal Customer Service (Return Policies, Answer Complaints, etc.)?**

Does your website answer all of the commonly asked questions with its FAQ section or offer easy-to-understand refund policies (or explicitly state that you don't offer refunds)? More about this in **Step 3: Converting Viewers into Clients**.

☐ **Make It Easy To Connect With You (Quickly)?**

Does it invite further engagement and seem like a place where people want to spend time? Does it reflect the personality and values of your business? Does it feel like your "virtual boutique"?

☐ ***Not* Look Like A Graveyard?**

Does it look like it's lively and up-to-date? Are the events listed already passed? Are the blog posts recent? Does it have a dated, out-of-style look?

☐ **Have a Google Business Page and a Google Analytics Account that You Can Check Regularly?**

If you've hired someone to build your site, are they setting up the Google Analytics? Are they willing to show you how to use it or refer you to someone who will? (Expect to pay extra for this training.)

☐ **Is It Set Up To Receive Technical Maintenance From Time To Time?**

Is there someone more technical than you whom you can turn to for assistance when your get out of your depth? Have you built it into your calendar to do testing every month or quarter to test links, forms, and shopping features and ensure that appropriate tools are updated and working fluidly?

Step Two
Understanding Your Audience

Primary Users

Creating User Avatars

Once you clearly understand your audience, building a website will actually be fairly easy. Your most important audience members are **primary users**—members of your target market. **Secondary users** include anyone else who might use your website, such as referral partners, media, strategic partners, potential employees, etc. (I go into more detail about this on page 20.) Understanding your users will determine everything: the copy; the design elements, including colors, photos, illustrations, and layout; media features like video; and the overall way the website flows and engages viewers.

The more you think of your users as real people with actual problems looking for solutions, the easier it will be to create your site. Most likely, you navigate websites differently than your parents do, so a website geared toward them might be very different than one designed to attract your attention.

Start by creating an avatar for each type of person you would consider a primary user. Write about each avatar as if it were a character in a story, complete with a name, an age, an income level, a job, and most importantly, a problem only your service or product can solve. Have fun with it—go into detail about her daily life. Does she have a dog? A boyfriend? Is she recently divorced? Tell us how she spends her day and where else she spends her money. How technical is she? How much money does she make? Did she go to college? What is her ethnicity or cultural background? What offering of yours would she be most interested in? What kinds of publications does she read? What does she like in a website? No-nonsense, straightforward content that gives her the information she is seeking and loads quickly, or does she want to experience the website, watch videos, read blog posts, and linger on the website before making a decision?

Avatar 1:

Avatar 2:

Avatar 3:

As each "person" considers interacting with your business, will it be a long-term relationship in which she will meet you or someone on your staff, or will you potentially never see her (as in a customer purchasing a necklace from your online store)? Consider whether she will appreciate seeing a picture of you (and other staff members) on the website. Will that compel her to buy something or book a session? Either way, you should seek to build a long-term, responsive relationship in which your website is revisited by your primary users subscribing to your newsletter, following you on social media, booking an appointment, making a purchase, or signing up for an event.

You will use all of this information beyond the launch of the website. Every time you want to add content to the site, you will want to consider your avatars. In fact, you may add features because you realize over time that you missed certain target primary users or delete or modify pages that aren't resonating with users or leading to a call to action.

Engaging Primary Users

Once you've written three character avatars, answer these questions:

1. What are three main segments of people you are seeking as clients? Within those categories, who specifically will be seeking those services? (*Example: "thirty-to-fifty-year-old women with school-aged children who are in a career transition" or "bass-fishing enthusiasts who are executive-level professionals"*)

a.

b.

c.

2. When you've determined these "most probable clients," ask yourself:

- What are their goals for seeking my product or service? What do they expect my product or service to do for them? (Will your counseling fix their marriage? Will your gadget keep them more organized?)

- What strong emotions are associated with successful engagement with my product or service?

- What are their hang-ups around hiring me or buying my product? What are they afraid of? What might cause them to hesitate?

- What are their pain points? This is different from hang-ups. Pain points are higher-level pain sources or goals, like, "I want to attract a different demographic to my business," or, "I want people to see my business as a warm, inviting neighborhood bakery," or, "I want to make better decisions in my career."

- What other services or products may they be looking for (that they either realize or don't realize)?

- How do I like people to approach me? For instance, in my case, people start with a free thirty-minute call or a one-hour session, or they call me directly (which usually results in one of the two other choices if they decide to proceed). How would I prefer to start relationships with my clients? How does this translate into a call to action?

- If there is some kind of call to action on the front page, what would that look like? For instance, I offer my free call on my home page. You might offer an email subscription button, a free download that offers tips or an excerpt from a book, or an event with a "Registration" button.

- Where do clients generally reside? Does my website speak to them? Is it culturally sensitive, and does it communicate appropriately? Should it be readable in more than one language? If so, how will you do this? Is the geographic region your website is intended to cover and serve clearly communicated? How can the site make this explicitly clear?

Diagram how you would like to lead each avatar to the call to action. Some avatars will potentially engage in more than one way, so diagram each alternative way.

Avatar 1:   Avatar 2:   Avatar 3:

Get a clearer picture of your ideal client by creating their vision board in this space, using magazine pictures and glue. (You can also use Pinterest.)

You'll return to considerations about engagement and competitors in **Step 5: Creating Dynamic Content**.

Secondary Users

Once you have your **primary users** dialed down, think about your **secondary users**. It may not be necessary to drill down to a high level of detail, but if you have specific referral partners or vendors who will see the website periodically, be thinking about what they might want to see on your website, too.

Following is a list of secondary users to consider:

- Referral Partners
- Blog or Newsletter Subscribers
- Future Clients
- Reporters/Media
- Vendors
- Employees
- Investors
- Influencers
- Reviewers
- Strategic Partners
- Affiliates

Out of all of these, I am recommending you consider **referral partners, blog or newsletter subscribers, future clients, reporters/media,** and **vendors** as you plan your website. If your website is planned well, the rest of the secondary users will either find the content compelling or not, but their engagement is not as critical, since, by default, they'll usually be reviewing your content with an understanding of the core audience you're trying to attract.

Referral Partners

Referral partners are professionals who will naturally refer business to you since your service often serves their clients' needs or helps them check some common task off their to-do list. Realtors will refer clients to landscapers and painters when a client wants to sell a house. If you make therapeutic foam rollers that people can incorporate into their yoga routine, acupuncturists and chiropractors will tell people about your website. Therapists will refer clients to me when their clients are frustrated with their careers or yearning to start a business.

You will want to think about referral partners when you think about your primary users, since they will be checking out your website to vet your services and products. Since therapists can be great referral partners for my business, I would want therapists to know that I have an MSW and see my website as calming, positive, and reassuring to their clients.

What do you want referral partners to know about your business? What questions might they have for you? How could you answer them?

Blog or Newsletter Subscribers

If you're planning to create a blog or newsletter, you will want to make it easy to find, keep it up-to-date, offer varied content, and answer questions that establish yourself as a thought leader in your industry. If you're not planning a blog or newsletter, you may still want to think through these questions since you may want to start one at some point.

Describe the content you will offer in one sentence. What questions will your newsletter answer? What questions will your blog answer? What are some things you are commonly asked? What are you curious about?

On what social media platform do you think your blog subscribers are most likely to share your content?

Future Clients

Think of your future clients as "warm leads." They may hire you or buy your product someday, but for now they are window-shopping. You will definitely want to keep in touch with them, though, since they may want to remember you but completely forget about you (despite their best intentions). This is why **a newsletter or blog can be a great way to stay in the forefront of their minds, but it's not the only way.** You can invite them to a closed Facebook group or a Meetup group or offer a download of a workbook excerpt or 10 percent off any product within the year in exchange for their email address. (Even if you send them a short email four times a year reminding them of your existence, you will vastly increase your potential to convert them into a client.)

What do you think future clients want to know about you right now? How often do you think they'd like to hear from you? *(Once a month? Every three months? Every six months?)*

Reporters/Media

If you cultivate robust content that answers compelling questions about trending topics, you will be more likely to attract media attention. This is another reason to keep your website fresh and relevant. If you have specific media outlets to attract, such as parenting magazines, stay up-to-date on the topics they tend to write about and vary your blog and newsletter content by season, as appropriate. The PR experts call media stories "earned media," which is more valuable than advertising since it is regarded with more credibility and is less likely to be skimmed.

What would you like reporters to write about your business? What expertise would you be excited to share with others? What would that look like (e.g., a podcast, a community news story, a magazine article)?

Vendors

You can potentially save prospective vendors (and yourself) time if you can answer their questions with your website content. For instance, if your salon only sells organic, cruelty-free hair care products, a prospective vendor who doesn't offer these products is not likely to reach out to you if these product standards are made clear on your website.

What do you want vendors to know about your business? What questions might they have for you? How could you answer them?

Engaging Secondary Users

For each of your potential secondary users, think about how you are trying to inform, convert, and/or engage viewers. Think about what the tools of engagement look like:

- Sale
- Subscription
- Demo Request
- Virtual Community/Closed Facebook Group
- Opt-in Email List
- Media Inquiry
- Employment Inquiry
- Investor Inquiry

List the secondary user types (including ones I didn't suggest before) who might visit your site:

From the list of secondary user types you generated, narrow your list to the top three you are most interested in attracting. Next, list the tools of engagement for each user.

Type of Secondary User
Therapist (example)

Engagement Tool(s)
Virtual Community

How does the website and/or engagement tool provide value for each of them?

Type of Secondary User

Therapists (example)

Value

Informational Resource

Don't Dismiss Your Brand

For those of you who don't find it necessary to brand yourself or your business, I might pose the questions, "Do you need to protect your reputation?" and, "Do you want to stand out among your competitors?" Or, if nothing else, "Do you want people to know how to refer business to you?"

Branding, in its simplest terms, enables potential clients to connect with you as quickly as possible. When people look at your site, its look and feel should dovetail with your other marketing materials and communicate your values, mission and ethos. If this seems overwhelming, rest assured that these considerations pay off over time.

Spend time developing a brand that thoughtfully communicates your values and messaging. Consult a branding expert or a graphic designer who specializes in branding. The core question when devising your brand is, "What strong emotions do I want associated with my business?" Focus on the problems you are solving for clients and how your approach differentiates you from the competition. This will help you build a website that easily communicates with your audience and effectively sells your services and products.

Step Three
Converting Visitors into Clients

Five "W"s and the "H"

In addition to thinking like a brick-and-mortar retailer, you'll want to also think like a journalist and cover the Five "W"s and the "H": **What, Why, When, Where, Who,** and **How**. This will help you think through every possible question viewers might have for your business as they compare you to the competition.

Answer these questions for each primary user avatar:

What about your purpose and mission attracts them?

Avatar 1: _____

Avatar 2: _____

Avatar 3: _____

Why would they pick you? Why would they choose your business over a competitor?

Avatar 1: _____

Avatar 2: _____

Avatar 3: _____

When are they going to engage with you? At what stage in their lives? On the weekends? Certain times of year? Certain holidays?

Avatar 1: _____

Avatar 2: _____

Avatar 3: _____

Where are they going to engage with you in person, if at all? Where are they going to engage with you on the website? Where on social media? (I consider blogs to be social media, by the way.)

Avatar 1:

in person: _____

website: _____

social media: _____

Avatar 2:

in person: _____

website: _____

social media: _____

Avatar 3:

in person: _____

website: _____

social media: _____

Who are they? Who do they want to be?

Avatar 1: _____

Avatar 2: _____

Avatar 3: _____

How are they going to engage? How are they going to stay connected?

Avatar 1: _____

Avatar 2: _____

Avatar 3: _____

Deeply Thinking the *Why*

The most important of these is arguably the **why**. When asking yourself why clients would pick you over competitor(s), be thoughtful and think carefully over each reason. (Don't be desperate to close every sale. If they are lured away too easily, they aren't your people. But if they are your people, consider what would compel them to stay. Price isn't usually why we buy—if we really want something, price is a minor consideration.)

Below are some questions to help you think through your why.

Come up with three compelling (not weak) reasons to pick you over the competition. Do you offer superior customer service? Are you willing to meet clients on Saturdays and evenings? Are you the best resume writer in town?

1. _____

2. _____

3. _____

Do you offer the opportunity for someone to feel like they're part of a tribe? If so, how? How do you keep them feeling like they're part of the tribe?

If you don't offer the "tribe" feeling, do you at least make them feel like you "get" them? How? How is this reflected in the design, colors, copy writing, illustrations, and photography?

Now think of three reasons they might pick your competitor over you:

1. _____

2. _____

3. _____

Play the Long Game and the Short Game

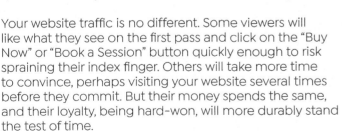

Let's return to that metaphor of your website as a brick-and-mortar store as you consider how most of us tend to shop in person. While some items jump off the shelf into our waiting arms the first time we enter a store, others take more consideration and repeated visits before we part with our hard-earned money.

Your website traffic is no different. Some viewers will like what they see on the first pass and click on the "Buy Now" or "Book a Session" button quickly enough to risk spraining their index finger. Others will take more time to convince, perhaps visiting your website several times before they commit. But their money spends the same, and their loyalty, being hard-won, will more durably stand the test of time.

If you create content to engage both kinds of consumers (and everyone between), you will build a website with robust content, strong SEO, and a potent ability to convert. This isn't about appealing to everyone—it's about

tailoring your content to a specific audience so well that they will feel like they have discovered something really special when they find your website.

Whether playing the short game or the long game, think of your conversion process for most users as the one-two-three punch of:

1. Research > 2. Engagement > 3. Decision

Every user who visits your site is doing **research**, whether trying to compare you to the competition, seeing what products and services exist in the first place, or stumbling upon your website by accident.

Once they are on your website, they will navigate it depending on:
• The feeling of connection with your brand
• Their readiness to purchase
• The level of complexity of the purchase
• Their familiarity with your industry
• The amount of time at their disposal

There are other factors, of course, but these five main "research navigation mindsets" will cover most website users. As you work through the questions that help you think about each style, be thinking about what will encourage deeper engagement. In the next chapter (Step 4: Building Your Architecture), you will consider the third decision "punch" as you design your landing pages with a definitive call to action.

For each of the research navigation mindsets, answer the following questions.

Connection to Brand

What types of writing will help you connect with your users? Formal business language in the third person? Conversational first-person writing that is warm and inviting?

What images and graphics will speak to your users? (Refer to your vision board for ideas.)

If you showcase personal bios of you or your employees, will they help people connect to you?

How will the pictures of you and employees achieve that?

Will you include a section that discusses what you care about or how your company was started—a list of core values or a history page?

What's another section you could include that would help your viewers connect to your brand?

If you do a blog, how will you draw readers in and convince them you're a brand worth following and telling others about?

What free downloadable PDF (e.g., 7 Ways to Stylishly Tie a Scarf or 3 Landscaping Designs for Small Backyards) will convince readers that you "get" them?

Level of Readiness

People will approach your website in varying levels of readiness. For career counseling, for instance, most people are A) starting their job, B) considering leaving their job, C) ready to quit their existing job, D) out of work, or E) wanting to reenter the workforce after an absence.

List the stages of readiness potential clients might be in as they work up to purchase mode.

As much as you can possibly guess, list the stages your potential customers could be experiencing. (Use as many spaces as you need, but if it exceeds nine, it's likely that two or more could be grouped into one.)

_____

_____

_____

_____

_____

_____

_____

_____

_____

_____

_____

_____

_____

_____

_____

_____

Level of Purchase Complexity

Some purchases are easier and faster than others. Some purchases are impulsive, and some require contemplation and comparison. We'll spend more time deliberating over car purchases and therapy services than gardening tools or throw pillows, as well we should.

In either case, the more examples you can give people that you're the right choice and the better able you are to establish a long-term relationship, the more likely you'll close the sale.

How much time do you think most people take before they decide to make a purchase? Does it vary by their state of readiness? If so, how? List the states of readiness from before and now also list how long each might take to make a purchase decision. What questions can you answer to move them closer to a decision?

State of Readiness Questions to Answer	Length of Decision
----------------------------	----------------------------
----------------------------	----------------------------
----------------------------	----------------------------
----------------------------	----------------------------
----------------------------	----------------------------
----------------------------	----------------------------
----------------------------	----------------------------
----------------------------	----------------------------
----------------------------	----------------------------
----------------------------	----------------------------

Familiarity with Your Industry

Customers will approach your industry and your service or product with differing levels of familiarity. Maybe your gardening store targets clients who are experienced gardeners and well-informed about shovels and seeds, but it's possible that some clients will be novices. The beginners and the pros and everyone between are going to navigate and research your site differently. Think about how you'll answer all of their concerns.

It's okay to speak to just one of these three levels of knowledge, but if you are expecting all of them, you won't want to talk down to the aficionados, and you definitely won't want to assume the beginners and moderately informed customers know more than they do. Take the opportunity to inform them, deepening your relationship with them. Think blogs, white papers, FAQ sections, newsletters, etc. Even your basic content pages can offer information that will make an impression, educate your clients, and potentially ease them closer to readiness.

What will beginners look like? How will your website speak to them?

What will moderately informed clients look like? How will your website speak to them?

What will well-informed clients look like? How will your website speak to them?

Amount of Disposable Time

Most of us have less disposable time than we'd like, but some have more than others. While disposable time is a factor that intersects with most of the other research navigation styles in some way, it looks a little different, depending on an individual's lifestyle, affluence, patience level, and occupation, etc. College students whose parents are footing the bill for their education, room, and board will have more time to peruse a website than a night-school student working part-time and raising three kids.

Consider how much time your clients have to get from contemplation to decision but make it easy for everyone to find your call to action. Since clients with more time may take that time to compare you to the competition, provide them with ways to spend time on your website to deepen engagement and pay attention to the tone of your content. People wanting to purchase quickly will appreciate a tone that is direct and to the point, while people with time to burn will appreciate a softer touch.

It's also possible that avatars will have different time sensitivities. My I-hate-my-job clients who know what kind of job they want are usually looking for someone to help turn around a resume quickly and racing to meet a job announcement deadline. My stay-at-home parents looking to reenter the workforce might call me the first day they find my website or wait more than a year before they reach out.

Will your clients appreciate a more straightforward, to-the-point approach or a warmer, spend-some-time-looking-around approach? Why do you think this?

As far as you can tell, will they visit your site several times before they contact you? If you answered yes, why do you think that?

Will you have clients who are more likely to reach out the first time they see your site? Why do you think that?

How will you engage people with less time? How will you engage those with more time?

Just the FAQs, Ma'am

Make sure every possible contingency has been considered and your customers always have a way to offer feedback or complaints. Incorporate an easy-to-understand return policy and respond to client comments as soon as possible. As your business grows, incorporate common questions into an FAQ section—this is also good for your SEO!

What are the questions people most commonly ask you about your business?

Bookmark this page. You'll return to this list of questions as you plan the architecture and navigation of your website in **Step 5: Creating Dynamic, Search-Optimized Content**.

Step Four
Building Your
Website Architecture

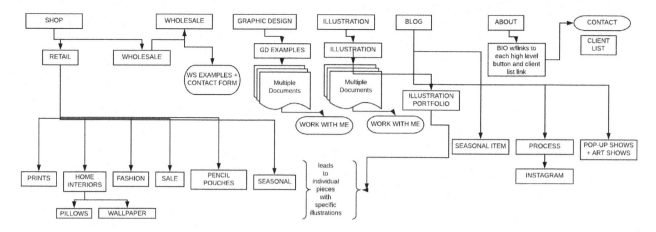

Website Architecture Defined

Website architecture is what it sounds like—the structure of your website. If you were building a store, you would start by building a framework to provide stability and shape to your creation. Website architecture is no different. It gives you a blueprint by which to guide the building (and maintenance) of your site to make sure nothing is forgotten and that the flow makes sense, leading people to the places they want to go and preventing them from getting trapped somewhere wondering how the heck they can get back the way they came in.

The best way to plan your architecture is to create a flowchart like you see above, to help dictate the flow of the website.

I'll go into more detail about the differing architecture styles in the **Architecture Design Patterns** section, but for now I'd like you to check off the main elements you would like to include in your launch. Rest assured you can always add more sections as you evolve. (You could plan to start a blog three months after launch, for instance.)

Website Elements Checklist

Check off the elements that you believe are critical to your site from day one:

- ☐ ABOUT
- ☐ BLOG
- ☐ CASE STUDIES
- ☐ CLIENT INTAKE PAPERWORK
- ☐ COMPANY HISTORY
- ☐ CONTACT
- ☐ GALLERY
- ☐ HOME
- ☐ PHILOSOPHY/APPROACH
- ☐ PORTFOLIO
- ☐ PRICING/RATES
- ☐ PRODUCTS
- ☐ RESOURCES
- ☐ SERVICES
- ☐ SHOP
- ☐ SHOPPING CART
- ☐ TESTIMONIALS

List any other sections you feel are critical to the launch of your website:

- ☐ _____ ☐ _____
- ☐ _____ ☐ _____
- ☐ _____ ☐ _____
- ☐ _____ ☐ _____
- ☐ _____ ☐ _____
- ☐ _____ ☐ _____

Architecture Design Patterns

Websites can look a thousand different ways, but I've stuck with a few basic architecture design patterns to give a sense of where to start. Like with a building, you could theoretically craft a blueprint for your website in an infinite number of ways, but the basic structures listed here will get you started. Each of these presented in a graphic is called a **site map**.

Like a flow chart, **a site map** simply lays out the pages in a way for your brain to keep track of what goes where. They can range from simple to complex and are the best way to communicate with a web developer or collaborator on how to build the site and how to manage its design as it grows.

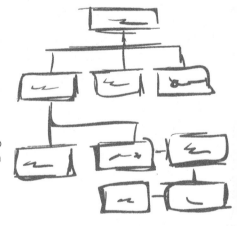

Splash Page

The **splash page** design is well-suited for projects with a specific focus and a limited amount of information. Business owners and event planners often use splash pages to announce the launch of a website, product, service, or event. Sometimes professionals will use splash pages that include contact information for their services as a prompt to download their vCard, which instantly inputs their information into a viewer's contact database. App developers will also use splash pages to give an at-a-glance snapshot of an app that leads users to an app store where they can find out more. If you google "website for an iPhone app" or "vCard web designs," you can find some interesting examples of splash pages.

One-Tier Structure

The **one-tier structure** puts all the pages on the same level and is commonly seen on brochure-style sites that showcase only a few pages. This site is only comfortable for the user if you have seven to nine elements. For larger sites with more pages, the navigation flow and content navigation quickly become unwieldy.

Two-Tiered Structure

The **two-tier structure** features a home page (or front page) with subpages. This structure consists of a home page that serves as a jumping-off point for all the other pages. The subpages have equal importance within the hierarchy but, again, should be limited to seven to nine pages to avoid organizational overwhelm.

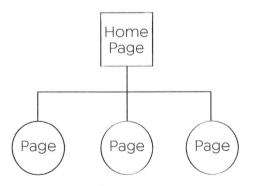

Three-Tier Structure (with a "Strict Hierarchy")

Some websites use a **Three-Tier Structure** of pages for their information design. On these sites, there will be a home page that links to subpages. Each subpage, or parent page, has its own subpages, or child pages. In this pattern, child pages are linked only from their parent page. This type of structure is said to have a **strict hierarchy** in which the website pages lead you down to the landing pages at the bottom.

First- and second-tier parent pages can also be called "high-level navigation" pages, while child pages are often called "low-level navigation" pages. A good rule of thumb is to never be any more than three clicks away from your home page.

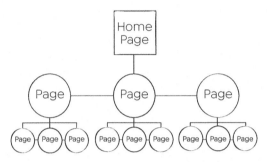

Three-Tier Structure (with a "Coexisting Hierarchy")

As an alternative to the strict hierarchy, this illustration demonstrates a **Three-Tier Structure** with a **coexisting hierarchy**. There are still parent and child pages, but in this case, child pages are accessible from multiple parent pages/higher-level pages. This is an efficient architecture plan if there is a lot of overlapping information on your site.

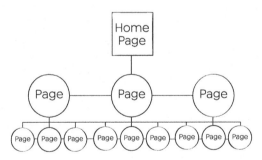

There are literally a thousand different ways to lay out a website, and these are just a few basic examples. Take a minute to sketch out the layout of a small website that you admire to get a feel for how a site map looks. Pick a small retailer in your neighborhood or a solo healthcare provider that you go to, like your dentist, acupuncturist, or naturopathic doctor. Use a square to represent the home page and circles to represent other pages, in keeping with the layouts above.

Your sketch of a small website:

Now take a stab at laying out your own website. Refer to your **Website Elements Checklist** on page 30 and play with how these pages might lead to one another in a logical way. Don't worry if it feels sloppy or "all over the place"—it probably will.

It's also likely that ideas for pages you hadn't thought of yet will pop into your head. That's okay. That's why this process is key to a well-planned website. You may think of transition pages you hadn't thought of before. For instance, maybe you thought to include a My Shop page but now it occurs to you each product will need to have an individual Product page featuring an image of the product and a "Buy Now" button.

Give yourself permission to play for now and don't get too hung up on whether it's unwieldy or confusing in its navigation. You will continue to sort it out as you think through your content. For now, just get something down on paper. *(Hint: Use a pencil.)* Now, go!

Your first sketch of your website:

Card Sort

Now, go back to your list of **Website Elements** from page 30, grab your sticky notes, and find a large surface like a white board or a piece of cardboard. Sticky notes are perfect for this process—I like clients to start with the smaller tab-size notes or the one-by-two-inch notes and then expand to the standard 2.5-by-2.5-inch size as they start to think through what each page will include.

1. First, write a website element on each sticky note. For instance, let's pretend that you're a therapist named Sally, and you decide you would like the following in your list of elements:

- Home
- Counseling for Individuals
- Counseling for Couples
- About
- Contact Me
- Mindfulness
- My Approach
- Rates
- Intake Forms

It could be that you could imagine some of these elements being incorporated on the same page—for instance, intake forms and rates could both show up on the About page, but it's useful to keep them separate for now, just so you can give yourself the freedom to play with different flow patterns.

2. Next, using the sticky notes and your large surface, start to sort your elements into a logical order. See the following example of how the therapist might start to organize her pages. Don't worry if it feels uncertain or open-ended. I have you use sticky notes for this step of the process to give you the option to rearrange pages as you start to think through the ways people will navigate your website. It's likely that you will rearrange pages several times before deciding on a final structure. But like you do when rearranging furniture in a room, trust that you will know when you've settled on the right pattern. And the fact that you have a site map will make it easier to change and plan for smart website growth.

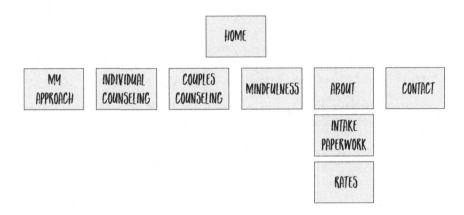

Now, start arranging your sticky notes. As you do so, keep the number of high-level navigation pages between three and nine and each number of child pages to two to seven per parent page. In the example, My Approach, Individual Counseling, Couples Counseling, Mindfulness, About, and Contact are all parent pages, and Intake Paperwork and Rates are child pages. Users will be able to access the Intake Paperwork and Rates pages from the About page, but for now, we're just going to tuck them under About. As we figure out the flow, we'll add arrows that suggest which pages lead to which, but for now, we're just trying to get a rough idea of how to organize the pages.

As Sally the therapist begins to lay out her pages, she realizes that she could minimize her number of high-level buttons by placing her services (Individual Counseling, Couples Counseling, and Mindfulness) under, well, a page called Services. If she decides this, she could sort her notes out to look like the graphic to the right:

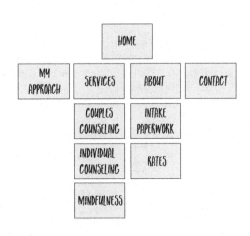

Keep in mind, as you lay out your notes, that each page should stand on its own as an individual page with content. Sally needs to ask herself, "What will my Services pages talk about?" Since she'd rather keep her counseling separate from her mindfulness treatment, which are offered exclusively in a group or retreat format, she decides on the following approach:

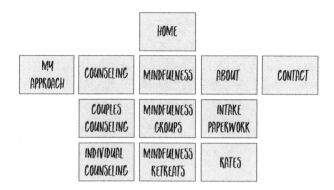

This is a basic overview and does not take into consideration the nuances of your website flow. We'll talk about that as we talk how you will want to triage website viewers—give them a choice that leads to another page or treat that page as a landing page.

Remember that a landing page is one that effectively leads to some type of engagement, like a **try**, **buy**, or **subscribe** option that either qualifies as a sale or potentially empowers the user to keep in touch or make a purchase. Refer back to the **try**, **buy**, or **subscribe** ideas you listed on page 12 as you consider how to structure your landing pages.

3. Go back to your sticky notes and see if you want to arrange them differently. Do you want to add any elements or pages you hadn't thought of? If you find yourself with more than seven child pages per parent page, can you group more than one page together or subdivide that parent page into two parent pages?

Think of your site as a house in which people will be asked to make a certain number of decisions (two to seven) before they enter another room, where they may be asked to make two to seven new decisions and then ultimately, once they've reached the landing page, feel encouraged to try, buy, or subscribe.

For instance, let's go back to Sally's website. Let's say she decided after all to add a Resources page. As she considers the resources she would like to recommend to clients, she creates the following list:

• Lines for Life
• Multnomah County Mental Health
• MBSR Portland
• Women's Crisis Line
• Liberation Institute
• Brightway Zen
• NAMI Oregon
• Portland Mindfulness
• Pause Meditation
• Morrison Child & Family Services

She wants to list these on a page labeled Resources but notices that her list might appeal to two different subsets of her target clientele—those seeking mental health services and those seeking mindfulness meditation guidance. She decides it might be more useful to her clients to separate the lists into Mental Health Resources and Mindfulness Resources, leading her to the following site map:

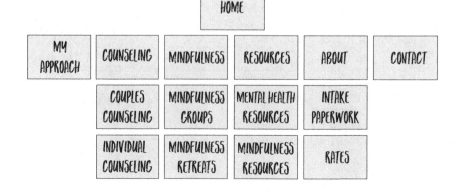

4. After you've gotten the pages of architecture laid out in a basic way with small sticky notes, switch to the larger (2.5 x 2.5) sticky notes, using three different colors.

This is why you will want a large surface like a white board, a large expanse of wall, or a table. Write the name of the page on the top of each sticky note, using one color for high-level pages and one color for the others:

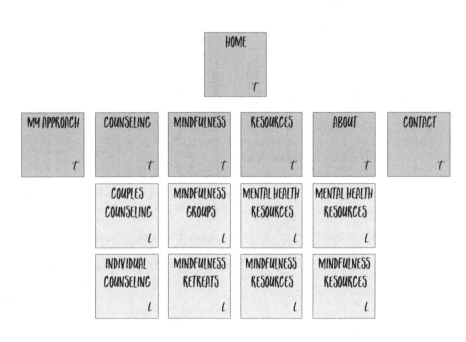

After you've arranged them to the point in which you're at least moderately satisfied, go through each sticky note and mark it with a "T" for "triage" and "L" for "landing page" in the lower right-hand corner of each note.

If you decide to include a third level of architecture, switch to the third color. Before you do so, space out the notes so that you can make room for your expanding architecture:

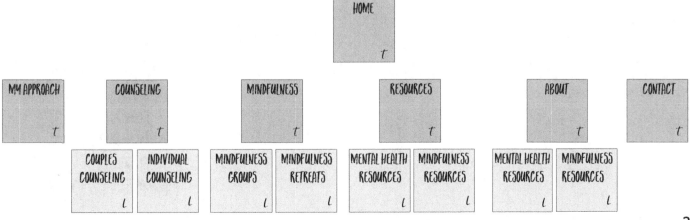

5. As you add the third layer (with a third color), group them under the second layer notes for now.
Don't worry about which pages will connect to which yet. We'll get to that. Also, change the letters "L" and "T," as needed. (Remember, the landing page is the last page clients are likely to visit before they decide to **try, buy,** or **subscribe**.)

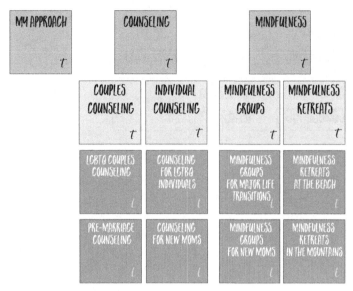

I have you switch to larger sticky notes for this process because I want you to take a minute to write on each one:

• A short outline of each page's content in bullet form
• A call to action on each note marked with an "L" (a call to action equals **try, buy,** or **subscribe**)

By the way, if you have great facility with online mind-mapping tools like LucidChart.com, MindMeister.com, or CardSmith.co, you could lay out your architecture on your computer. I just like sticky notes and large surfaces because I think it gives our brain a chance to interact with the information in a more playful, spontaneous way that helps create better results. Go with the process that helps your brain feel the most nimble and creative. If you do prefer a digital tool for this step, my highest recommendation goes to CardSmith, which most closely mimics sticky notes and lets you expand your "notes" and include to-do lists, images, and icons.

Mindfulness Resources

Introductory Paragraph
☐ Write Mindfulness Resources intro paragraph

Local Mindfulness Resources:
MBSR Portland
Brightway Zen
Portland Mindfulness
Positivity Meditation
Sally's Mindfulness Retreat*

l

6. As you roughly outline your pages on these sticky notes, think about how the pages might refer to other pages within your structure.

As Sally the therapist works out her architecture, she realizes that she may want to add her own mindfulness retreat among her mindfulness resources, so she finds it helpful to list **Sally's Mindfulness Retreat** on her **Mindfulness Resources** sticky note and place an asterisk next to it indicating that it will link to something internal in her website. She also could add to-do lists to keep her on track. To plan out this page, she could have a sticky note that looks like the image to the left.

Sally will leave an "L" on this sticky note since this page will remain a landing page, even though it includes internal links to other pages. She will want to think about how she hopes to engage people with her with a **try, buy,** or **subscribe** option. For pages that include resources, I recommend a try or subscribe option—Sally could offer a downloadable list of mindfulness resources or mindfulness tips as a try option or a mindfulness newsletter and a short form with a "Subscribe" button. Either way, this option should appear in a sidebar since not everyone will scroll to the bottom of the page if it's too lengthy.

Sally may find that her **About** page will also circle back to several other pages in her structure, leading people to explore her **Counseling** page or her **Resources** page.

Again, this page still remains a landing (L) page and should have a way for people to contact Sally directly. There is a case to be made that both an About page and a Contact page could be redundant. Having people beta test your website can provide better insight into these sorts of decisions.

ABOUT
[SHORT BIO PARAGRAPH]
- MY APPROACH
- COUNSELING SERVICES*
- MINDFULNESS*
- RESOURCES*
[CONTACT INFORMATION]   *l*

7. To plan more in-depth content for each page, use Microsoft Word or Pages before you start your website. I recommend using a separate Word or Pages file for each page of the website and organizing it in specific folders to correlate with the higher-level buttons.

As Sally builds her content, she can have folders on her hard drive or in Dropbox cloud storage titled **My Approach, Counseling, Mindfulness, Resources, About,** and **Contact** and place files in each folder that are titled by their page name.

8. Keep rearranging your sticky notes until you're completely satisfied with the architecture. It may still change after you start writing the content more fully, but at least you will have a point of reference to keep you organized and on track. Draw your final or close-to-final flowchart out on a tool like LucidChart, Mindmeister, or Cardsmith, complete with arrows to indicate the flow of the website. I've even used Excel for this step, but since my friend Monica created CardSmith (and I love it), I used it to create this flowchart:

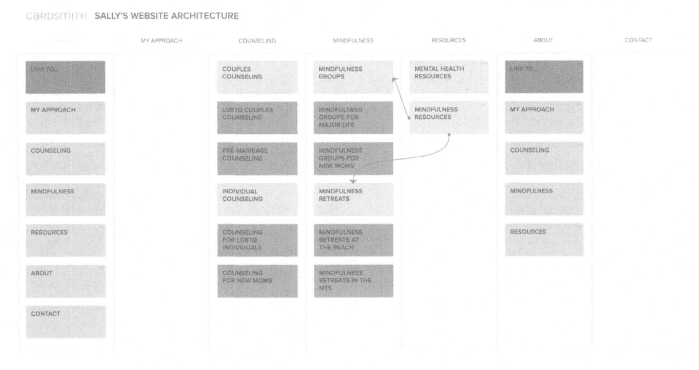

Like the sticky-note approach, this flowchart uses the color to indicate the level of architecture (Medium Gray=1st, Light Gray=2nd, and Dark Gray=3rd). If you want to "kick it old school," you can draw your final flowchart on a piece of paper, but be sure to create something you can post on a wall in a room where you tend to work on your website. If you're like me and tend to work in different places, make sure your final flowchart is something you can take with you no matter where you go.

Architectural Strategy
(Things to Keep in Mind)

While I've walked you through one example of planning a website, there's no way to really "get it" until you start playing around with it yourself. Pay attention to other websites and how they flow and where your reaction lies on the continuum between pleasant and confusing. Tune in to whether websites you frequently surf employ landing pages effectively and how compelling their calls to action are. **Here are a few things to keep in mind:**

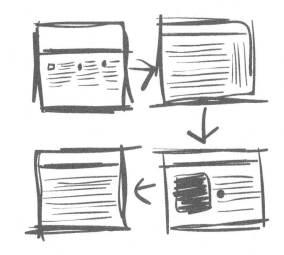

1. Purchase navigation needs to be clear, work quickly, and offer a confirmation page. We've all spent time on those websites that hide the shopping cart or use a confusing, unwieldy online purchasing form with distracting graphics. Make it as easy as possible for clients to buy from you. Test all of your links repeatedly and ask your friends to test it and provide feedback. Appeal to your most detail-oriented friends' competitive streaks and offer them a buck for every broken link they find first.

2. Think through how you're leading people to a call to action. If you think of your website like a store, as I suggested in Step 1: Preplanning Your Website, you'll want to consider how long you want people to linger before they perform a call to action. Go back to the page and reconsider your diagram of call-to-action engagement.

For some people, maybe they visit your website and subscribe to your newsletter, and after a few weeks, they receive your newsletter and see that you're hosting a workshop—then they return and register for the workshop.

For someone else, they might visit your website the first time, like what they see and book a session.

Who do you want to accommodate? Both of them! But before you start your architecture, you're going to want to understand how they might be navigating your website and give them chances at various places to engage or act (buy, try, or subscribe)—and you will want to do so without seeming too needy. Just like a retailer sometimes needs to back off, you need to have nice things to look at but not breathe down a visitor's neck for fear of scaring them off.

3. Start with the pain points. Take each user from the motivations that led them to your website and lead them where you want them to go. For instance, someone visiting my SparkaCareer.com website might say, *"I'm curious about career counseling but have never tried it before,"* and click on the "Career Counseling" button. I try to answer their questions and then offer options for the types of counseling career counseling areas I specialize in: advancement, balance, transition, and workforce reentry.

Next, I offer a breakdown of each of the packages I offer for these four main areas and two calls to action—a button to set up a free thirty-minute phone call and a button to schedule a one-hour session with me.

If you consider all of the possible questions your ideal clients might have while navigating your website and answer them as well as you can, you're more likely to create an experience that leads to engagement. Different people have varying levels of patience with reading, so it's important to tune in to your audience but err on the side of brevity.

4. Build SEO into your architecture but don't ever think that you're "finished." Brainstorm a list of keywords before you start planning your architecture so that you can be mindful of the terms you will want to integrate. Ask for help with this process from someone who exemplifies your ideal client. Strategically consider how an ideal client searching for your services and products would search for a solution on Google. Go back to the **pain points** you identified on page TK.

The higher the level of the word or phrase in your architecture, the more weight it will hold. The names of pages will be your **header (or H1)** tags, and they are the most sacred. Higher-level pages (like **Counseling** and **Mindfulness** for Sally) will possess the most heft. The hierarchy will descend from there, but you will also be able to build SEO strength with **subhead (H2 and H3)** tags. This will give you the chance to work keywords into your content, but you want to balance that with a writing flow that makes sense and provides useful information.

Links to other pages on your website (inbound links) and to external websites (outbound links), bulleted lists of important keywords, photographs and video with "alt" tags that include keywords, and strategically written, timely blog posts are a few other ways to augment your SEO.

Since Google likes your website to grow and offer consistently fresh content, a blog is the best way to consistently enhance your SEO. You will also build credibility in your industry, answer questions that keep your users engaged, and continue to add keywords to bolster your search engine ranking.

True search engine optimization is full of several nuances, so consider consulting with an SEO expert in order to achieve meaningful results (or be willing to dive deeper into understanding it yourself). It's not rocket science, and once you understand it, it pays huge dividends for the time invested.

Overall, the best strategy to optimize your website for both search engines and repeated viewers is to provide compelling, relevant content that flows logically, provides solutions to pain points, and pleases the eye on all platforms (laptops, smart phones, tablets, etc.).

Keyword List Brainstorm:

Step Five
Creating Dynamic, Search-Optimized Content

SEO Basics

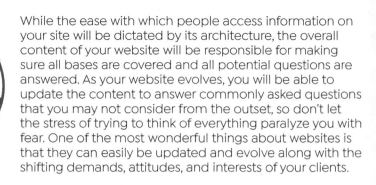

Once you have a general idea of how to lay out your website, you can start to nail down the content of your website. The term **content** generally refers to any copy, blog posts, contact or forms, PDF downloads—anything, basically, that your website is offering for viewers to engage and convert them into clients.

You may have already started to write some pages for your website, which is great. I ask you to carefully plan out your architecture first because I think it makes it easier to effectively create and organize your content if you know where it will most easily be found and lead your prospects to the intended destination of your landing page.

As I've mentioned, with some websites, this will be a lead-me-to-the-information-as-quickly-as-possible proposition. Pizza places are a great example of this—when most people look up a pizza place online, they are looking for a menu to see what kinds of pizza they offer and a phone number to call to order their pie.

On the other extreme are let-me-spend-some-time-getting-to-know-a-bit-about-your-business-before-I-commit propositions. This is demonstrated well by an intelligently constructed health-practice website. People are generally more thoughtful about where they seek out their wellness services than where they order pizza (hopefully). They will appreciate seeing photos of practitioners, absorbing their philosophies, reviewing their educational and professional backgrounds, understanding the methods and expectations of their practice, and reading their reviews.

There will, of course, be businesses that fall between these two ends of the time-expenditure continuum, and even for the businesses that are expected to share more information to facilitate a client conversion, basic information should always be easily and quickly found—hours of operation, contact information, and location are a few examples.

Consider the things you often tell people to find on your site before they engage—paperwork that needs to be filled out or signed, events that require payment and registration to attend, or the page of your online shop that includes a popular item. Make sure these things can be found easily with one click or fewer from the home page.

While the ease with which people access information on your site will be dictated by its architecture, the overall content of your website will be responsible for making sure all bases are covered and all potential questions are answered. As your website evolves, you will be able to update the content to answer commonly asked questions that you may not consider from the outset, so don't let the stress of trying to think of everything paralyze you with fear. One of the most wonderful things about websites is that they can easily be updated and evolve along with the shifting demands, attitudes, and interests of your clients.

Content Brainstorming

In **Step 4: Building Your Website Architecture**, I asked you to check off a list of website elements that you want to include in your website and then use sticky notes to arrange them in the order of your intended navigation.

Refer to the final architectural flowchart you were prompted to create in **Step 4** and list the elements in the chart here. After you've listed them, give each one an abbreviation. An About Us page could be given the abbreviation "AU," for instance. Then indicate with "Yes" or "No" if that page is a triage or landing page. (If you're not sure yet, write "DN" for "Don't Know.")

Content Brainstorm List

Website Element:	Abbreviation:	Triage:	Landing:
Example: About Us	AU	Yes	No

How to Plan and Organize Your Content

If you are like most people, some pages of your website will flow out of your mind with ease, feel like they "write themselves," and perfectly express your thoughts with clarity and precision, while other pages may not come as readily or, on the first reading, may sound awkward and forced. When this happens, your best bet is to push through it, take a break from it, and then revisit it with fresh eyes.

If writer's block is paralyzing you, see if outlining the content for your page helps, giving you the chance to organize your thoughts and create a structure that makes sense. Outlining your pages before you write them also ensures that you will cover all of the content you are hoping to share and potentially break information into sections with subheads that ease the reader's eye to the information they are seeking.

For each page that you write, a good rule of thumb is to create a separate folder for each high-level navigation button on your page and a distinct Word file for each page. Then sort each on your hard drive into the appropriate high-level-button folder. This keeps your pages from getting muddled and ensures that you can readily find your content when needed.

If you are less of a digital thinker and prefer a tangible representation of your organizational plan, create a binder with tabs that represent each high-level button in addition to your online files. Keep a copy of your architecture plan in this binder as well and include a clear plastic sheet protector for each tab to collect photos from magazines that inspire you. These plastic sheets will be great resources when you start visiting stock imagery sites looking for photos. (If you're using digital resources exclusively to plan your content, include a subfolder within each high-level-button folder to collect image ideas. You could also use Pinterest, if inclined, to collect and organize images.

As you write your content, give yourself permission to write things out of order. Write the content that comes most easily first and leave the more difficult writing at the end of the process. There are no rules about what order in which to write your content, and you will feel more productive if you are writing rather than not creating any content. If necessary, give yourself permission to hire a website content writer. These angels do exist, and they can help you unlock your thoughts and write content for your intended audience.

Before you hire a writer, though, write as much of the content as you possibly can and, at a minimum, outline the content that has you stumped. The writer will appreciate this enormously (and it will save you money).

On page 43, I provide some prompts for pages typically found on most websites to get you started. Use these prompts to help you generate your content. If you find these prompts work for you, try writing prompts for yourself to pry out content for the more challenging pages.

SEO Matters

If your pages aren't optimized to mention what your products/services are, then they're not going to be found...The search engines can only work with the data you give them...You need to help them to help you, and that's where SEO comes into play. —Rebecca Murtagh, author of *Million Dollar Websites*

While I want you to plan and organize your content to fully consider SEO and augment your site's ability to be found, your main objective is to build the best possible website with easy-to-find, useful, high-quality information that stands out from your competitors. If you do this, and carefully construct your website with an eye toward keywords and UX/UI design, you should be in excellent shape with your Google ranking.

Keyword Review

Step 4: Building Your Website Architecture provided a quick primer on SEO considerations in regard to your website structure, including headers and subheads and their corresponding tags (H1, H2, H3, etc.). As mentioned previously, however, if you create robust content in your website overall, that is the best way to attract the prospective clients and viewers who are fervently (or calmly) searching on Google for the services and problem-solving products you want to sell.

1. Go back to your Keyword List Brainstorm on page 38. Write all of the keywords and keyword phrases again that you still believe to be potentially popular search terms for your prospective clients. (This may seem redundant, but there is a method to my madness.) Are there any keywords you could add to your list? If so, list them too.

2. Return to the list of commonly asked questions for your business in the Just the FAQs section on page 28. Use a highlighter to pick out the keywords and keyword phrases from your list of questions that seem to pop out at you as words that are potentially popular search terms for your prospective clients. List the words that seem like robust keywords:

3. Use the Google Keyword Planner to prompt ideas for words you may have overlooked. Visit https://ads.google.com/home/tools/keyword-planner/ and click on the blue "Go to Keyword Planner" button. On the next page, click on "Discover new keywords" and list your business type (yoga studio, counseling clinic, etc.) under "Enter products or services closely related to your business." You will see a page that looks like a spreadsheet called a Keyword Plan and ranks keywords and keyword phrases by the frequency of searches (listed under "Avg. monthly

Resist the temptation to spend too much time with the Keyword Planner tool. Your best search terms will come from the phrase or word most commonly used to describe your business. Try to think like your client as she is searching for your services. Although you may offer DBT to treat PTSD symptoms in your clients, your prospective client may be searching for "trauma counselors."

Focus on what makes you unique. Maybe you own a cheese shop that sells local artisan cheeses and is the only place in town that sells locally crafted burrata along with a range of distinctive, hard-to-find selections. Someone could be typing "burrata" and the name of your city. A page on your site like Unique Cheeses or even Cheese Varieties that lists "burrata" with an H2 subhead and expounds on its virtues would send this creamy-mozzarella lover over the moon.

searches"). Click on "DOWNLOAD KEYWORD IDEAS" to generate this list as an Excel file and comb through it. List keyword ideas that you would like your website to include. You can even play with the Keyword Planner for more specific ideas, if you believe it would be helpful. For instance, a counselor who offered career counseling might add the word "career" to "counseling" to see what other keywords and keyword phrases pop up that they had not already considered, such as "career assessments" or "life coaching".

4. Go back through these three lists of keywords and compare it to your Website Elements Checklist on page 30. Next to each keyword, list the code for the element(s) to which it seems to most closely correlate.

For instance, let's say your business is a yoga studio, and "muscle tone" made one of your final lists of keyword phrases, and your list of elements includes "blog" (with the abbreviation of "B") and a page called Benefits of Yoga (with the abbreviation of "BoY"). You could then write a "B, BoY" next to the keyword phrase "muscle tone."

muscle tone (B, BoY)

As you write the final copy for your website, you can refer to this keyword list and have a way to quickly reference words that you will want to incorporate into your content. As you write your About Us page (abbreviated with "AU"), you can scan your list of keywords and keyword phrases to see which ones have "AU" next to them to ensure that you are thoroughly integrating the greatest number of SEO-friendly words into your content.

SEO Copywriting Tips

While well-placed and frequent use of keywords will improve your website's search engine rank, the best way to optimize searchability is to simply write robust, dynamic content that is easy to read, concise, and well-organized. Following are a few guidelines to get you started.

1. Use an active, not passive, voice. In an active voice, the subject of the sentence performs the action instead of receiving the action:

Active: The business coach taught five modules of her practice management course.
Passive: Five modules of a practice management course were taught by the business coach.

2. Write clear, brief paragraphs, starting with the most important sentence, and try to limit your paragraphs to three or four sentences. If they must be longer, six or seven sentences is plenty.

3. Write short sentences. If you must write longer sentences, keep them to twenty words, since shorter sentences are easier to read than longer ones and less likely to have grammatical errors.

4. Limit your use of arcane or challenging words. Avoid words that require an advanced vocabulary or have too many syllables. You can break this rule, however, if your website deals with heady, scientific, highly technical topics. If a difficult word looms largely in your keyword research, you should obviously use it, but keep the writing as lively and accessible as possible.

5. Use transition words intelligently. Used well, transition words like "because" or "however" provide direction for your readers and contribute to your copy's flow. If summarizing, use "first," "second," etc. If comparing, try "same," "rather," or "either." When concluding, use "therefore" or "consequently."

6. Use online readability scanners. SEO plug-ins offered by companies like Yoast.com have built-in tools to assess the readability of your writing, providing a score to help you streamline your writing flow. Once your site is live, you can plug in your URL to a readability scanner like www.webfx.com to ascertain readability.

Content Prompts for Specific Pages

As promised, I have listed some prompts for the main pages that exist on most websites. Use these to help you generate language for your pages. This is meant to keep you from getting stuck and help you think through every thought you may want to include. From the outset, don't worry about being too wordy. You can always go back and prune your content. For now, give yourself the chance to express everything you are thinking. Use bullet points if it helps you organize your thoughts. Trust the process.

HOME PAGE

If you had three minutes to tell people about your business and leave a lasting impression, what would you say?

What is the goal of your home page? (Lead people further into the site? Invite them to sign up for an event? Make mouths water when viewers see pictures of your café's food? Establish yourself as a lawyer who is at once professional yet warm and approachable?)

What are the top three services or products your target clients are looking for when they come to your website?

1.

2.

3.

What could you say to them to convey that they have landed on the right page?

Once they know a bit about you, what are the five main questions they would want answered if they returned to your website (how to contact you, what hours you are open, when your next event is scheduled, etc.)**?**

1.

2.

3.

4.

5.

What are some keywords that you will want to be certain to include on the home page?

What are the questions or phrases to pose to get them to explore other pages that will lead them to landing pages?

What value does your business offer over and above your competitors?

What makes you stand out from competitors?

If you as an individual are your brand, what sets you apart from competitors?

How would others describe your brand?

What is your business proposition? What problems do you propose to solve? What makes your approach unique?

How would you like people to describe your business?

What social media platforms would you like to invite users to follow?

How would you like them to contact you? (e.g., contact form, phone, email)

ABOUT PAGE

What makes your business unique?

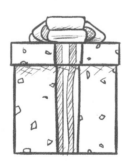

What call to action makes the most sense to include on this page (e.g., contact form, phone number, download of ten tips for setting up an online dating profile)?

SERVICES PAGE

What are your main service offerings?

Describe each of your services in one sentence or phrase in a way that makes them sound like something your target client could never turn down (e.g., "Couples counseling that helps you reconnect and find the joy your relationship has been missing").

What call to action makes the most sense to include on this page?

If you have more than seven services, is there a way to subcategorize your services?

PRODUCTS PAGE

What are your main product offerings?

If you have more than seven products, is there a way to subcategorize them into a few product lines?

How would you like people to describe your services?

How would you like people to describe your products?

What call to action makes the most sense to include on this page?

What call to action makes the most sense to include on this page?

Describe each of your products in one sentence or phrase in a way that makes them sound like something your target client could never turn down (e.g., *"Jane's Jasmine-Infused CBD Massage Oil will make you forget the terrible day you just had and will invite your mind and body to feel renewed and refreshed."*).

What call to action makes the most sense to include on this page?

CONTACT PAGE

What do you want your clients to know about before they contact you?

What contact information do you want to share? (If you don't want phone calls, don't include a phone number. If you can't respond to every email within twenty-four to forty-eight hours, find a way to automate responses to explain the delay or invite another form of engagement. If you don't want them to know where your business is located, don't include the address or only include a mailing address.)

What are all the questions they might pick up the phone to ask that could be answered on the contact page (e.g., parking, product returns, hours of operation, rates and pricing, directions)**?**

What social media platforms would you like to invite users to follow?

What call to action makes the most sense to include on this page?

Convert Your Prompts to Copy

Now revisit the prompts from each section and start to write cohesive copy for your website pages. Pay attention to the keywords that will potentially optimize your website for Google searches and thread them throughout your content. Keep your content well-organized and divided into folders and subfolders that reflect the architecture of your website. This will make your copy easy to retrieve as you start to work on your website (or delegate the building of your website to a professional).

Hold off on showing your copy to anyone else unless they know your business well or are experienced website copywriters who understand SEO and can provide helpful pointers. Keep in mind that your most valuable keywords will perform better when they are in headings and subheadings on your pages and showing up in lists of bullet points.

The best strategy for your SEO and your brand, however, will always be well-written, informative, robust content. Make sure your writing is readable and enjoyable to your target clients and referral partners, engages and informs viewers, and reflects your brand in a flattering, distinctive way. You will be way ahead of the game, especially if the flow of your site is easy to navigate and invites viewers to a landing page that converts viewers to clients.

Step Six
Getting Your Website Built

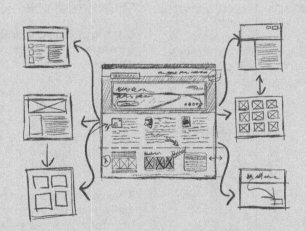

To DIY (Do-It-Yourself) or Not to DIY

By this stage, you may not have all of your website content completely written and figured out, but hopefully you will feel ready to start thinking about putting a website together. I hope this workbook has proven helpful in helping you generate content and think strategically about how your website can convert viewers into customers.

The big decision at this point is to determine whether you will build the website yourself or hire someone to build it for you. Whatever your decision, by completing all of this workbook's exercises and carefully considering your architecture, you will be way ahead of most clients who approach website developers—usually with an idea in their head or a few scribbles on a notepad but little else to show in the way of content or an architectural format.

While I can't make this decision for you, I can offer some pros and cons to both approaches. This chapter also briefly overviews website-building platforms like WordPress, Wix, and Squarespace. While there are dozens of other platforms, these are the most commonly used and the ones I most highly recommend.

There are merits to the DIY (do-it-yourself) and the hiring-a-pro approaches. Don't dismiss the thought of a hybrid approach in which you could hire someone to help you get the framework started and train you to update the site and add pages over time. In either case, I recommend that you build a baseline working knowledge of how your site works so that you can engage with it as needed as your business grows and protect it from hacking and crashes. More importantly, should your website face sabotage or other threats, your ability to respond effectively will depend on your willingness to gain some basic technical expertise.

The PROs of Building Your Site Yourself

The best reason to build your website yourself is that there is no feeling that can compare with the satisfaction of knowing how every inch of your website is constructed. You will be able to update it when you want without hiring a professional and paying (and then waiting) for those changes. Here are a few more reasons to take on the challenge of website development.

1. It will save you hundreds, possibly thousands, of dollars. If this is the only motivator, it may not be enough. Money can quickly be absorbed in the form of time lost working on other aspects of your business or serving clients, so be really certain that building your website will not completely suck your will to live. If you are confident that you have enough technical skills to meet the challenge, trying your hand at building a website is a worthwhile proposition. If you are less confident in your technical skills but fairly certain your end product will contain fifteen pages or fewer, I recommend you give DIY a try.

2. You will be able to make updates quickly and easily. Nothing feels as good as controlling when and how to make changes on your website without the use of an intermediary you may need to wait on or who could charge you more than you expected. If you don't think you will want to make changes yourself, this perk may not move the needle for you. (You can hire professionals who will train you on how to update your site. They may charge extra, but the expense could be worth it.)

3. You can build the site at your own pace. If you do not have a hard, fast deadline for launching your website, building it yourself can give you time to make solid decisions and create a site you are proud to associate with your business. If procrastination is a constant challenge for you, however, you may benefit from a deadline-driven professional.

4. You will add a valuable skill to your skill set. It is never a waste of time to add web development and SEO skills to your resume. You will also feel more in control of other technical aspects of your business once you have mastered this highly sought-after skill.

5. You can change directions midstream more easily. If you decide midway through the development phase to add a small e-commerce component to your website, a website developer will charge you significant fees to change direction. If you know you are prone to changing your mind, keeping the costs under control may work in your favor. (A case can be made, however, that a website developer will keep you on track if your indecisiveness runs the risk of delaying completion of your website indefinitely.)

6. Integrating your online presence with social media will be easier. If you plan to use social media to promote your website and your business, your social media marketing will be more seamless if you build the website yourself. You can always hire social media professionals, but few website professionals are highly versed in social media too. Since social media is more successful with a personal touch, you will be more in control of your social media brand if you understand how to integrate your social media platforms with your website.

7. No one knows your business or your target clients as well as you do. You are the best resource for understanding how to create a website that speaks to your clients. You fully appreciate how to motivate and inspire them and choose imagery and graphics that create connection and response. You can still convey this depth of understanding to a website developer, but you will need to take the time to hire someone who fully appreciates the nuances of your target market and your field. This is certainly possible but will take time and due diligence.

8. You can always find someone to fix your website if you hit a brick wall. If you are really on the fence about whether or not to hire someone, you could give it a go and hire someone if you get into the weeds. It can be smart for even the most tech-savvy business owner to have a professional at the ready should things go haywire or you find yourself wanting to add bells and whistles (like video integration, for example).

The CONs of Building Your Site Yourself

While there are several perks to building your own site, there are definitely things to consider, too. Below are some of the factors to consider as you weigh your options.

1. It may take you longer. If you are technologically proficient and have built a website before, this will not be as big of hurdle. But if you have to learn new skills and feel uncertain about your capacity to navigate technical challenges, building a website yourself may take longer than hiring a pro. (Then again, if you have to wait for a pro with a long waitlist and are in a hurry to get your site up, you may be better off getting started yourself, especially if your website is fewer than fifteen pages.)

2. You will have to make all of the decisions yourself. This may seem like a strange con if you like being in control, but there will be times when a pro can help you navigate tough decisions. The more complex the architecture of your website, the more likely hiring a pro is a good idea. If you have a business partner or accountability partner, this person can also serve as a sounding board and/or a project manager.

3. You might find yourself dangerously delayed if you don't know how to do something or fix a problem. If your default mechanism is psychological paralysis when faced with complex challenges, it may serve you to hire a professional. If, however, you can be relied upon to muddle through tricky situations and you enjoy finding creative solutions and figuring things out, you may be a natural website developer.

4. The money you save may get absorbed by the time you spend figuring out things that are beyond your ken. While it can be satisfying to find solutions to complicated snags along the way, you can easily find yourself losing time (and money) if you get too stubborn about seeking out expertise when you need it. Know when to ask for help. Don't burn too much time when hiring a professional can solve a problem in a few hours or less.

5. You may be too close to your business to truly appreciate the outsider perspective. While you may know your clients better than anyone, you may be too close to your professional expertise to know how to translate your industry jargon into language that persuades and converts. If you have a background in marketing or appreciate how to empathize and communicate with prospective clients, this may not be an issue, but it can still serve you to have objective outsiders give you candid perspectives on how your site communicates your message and leads viewers to the all-important landing page(s).

6. The final product may look unprofessional. This is less an issue every day with the advent and continuous improvement of web development tools, but you will, again, want to consult objective outsiders with graphic design chops to give you their honest feedback on the final result.

7. Launching your website will be more challenging. A website developer worth his or her salt will make sure that no links are broken, your website platform is protected from viruses and hacks, and that your SEO is in order, just to name a few launch checklist items. Whether you hire a pro or not, make sure your site is sufficiently beta-tested, proofread for typos and grammatical errors, and something that reflects your business as well as possible.

8. Your inner critic may get in the way. This may happen whether you hire a pro or do it yourself, but if your inner critic has a tendency to keep you from finishing projects, hire a pro or, at a minimum, hire a project manager to help you keep the trains running on time. Try not to let the perfect be the enemy of the good—the great thing about websites is that they can always be updated and improved.

The PROs of Hiring a Pro

The best reason to hire a pro to build your website is that it frees you up to focus on other aspects of your business. Here are a few more reasons to consider hiring a professional website developer.

1. They will (most likely) do it faster. Competent website developers will have the experience and the team to create and launch your site more quickly than you will. When screening web developers, ask if you can speak to past customers and be clear about your expectations and timeline. Remember, however, that they will also rely on you to respond to their correspondence to keep the project on track and that significant changes to the project scope will delay launch.

2. They will have the tools they need to make everything work smoothly and fix problems quickly. The better you understand everything you want your website to do, the easier it will be to screen for the right developer. If you know you want to incorporate social media feeds from Facebook and Instagram, ask the developer about their experience with social media integration tools. The better prepared you are, the happier you will be with your choice of developer.

3. You can hire someone with an impressive body of work, and the final product will look professional. You can carefully review the portfolio of prospective developers to see if they can handle your project. If you are impressed by their work (and their business website), it is likely that they can create a website you will feel good about. When reviewing their past work, look for all of the features you are hoping to implement in your site, and now that you know something about architecture, ask yourself, Does this website effectively convert clients? Can I find everything I'm looking for? Does it answer my questions? Don't forget SEO—search for the developer's services and products on Google to see how they rank.

4. You can hire a web developer with SEO expertise. If you want to make sure your SEO is robust from the start, I recommend hiring a website developer who is well-versed in SEO strategy or at least has a working relationship with an SEO consultant.

5. You will have a professional to consult when you face tough decisions about your architecture or graphics. This point is not to be underestimated. It can feel overwhelming to make big decisions about your architecture, graphics, social media, and other major considerations. Having a professional you trust to consult and talk through important conundrums about your website can be extremely beneficial, especially if your website has a complicated architecture and more than three landing pages.

6. You will have a professional to secure a successful website launch. This is a critical step of the process and not to be underestimated in its scope and complexity. You will want to make sure people are beta-testing your website, not just to make sure the navigation is sensible and elegant but to ensure that there are no broken links or images, no videos or images that are taking too long to load, no glaring errors that would cause you embarrassment, and maximum protection from viruses and hackers. When screening professionals, ask them about their beta-testing and launch processes. If they dodge these questions or fail to answer them to your standards, move on to the next candidate.

7. A pro will know how to build in protections to keep your site secure from hacking and viruses. This is a key consideration not just for launch but for the duration of your website. You should make sure that your site is continuously protected from vulnerabilities and talk with your website developer about how best to keep your site safe from corruption.

The CONs of Hiring a Pro

Hiring a professional website developer has its complications, too. Above all, you will want to clearly maintain control of your domain and host – broken record that I may be – and be thorough in the vetting process and clear and consistent in your expectations from your developer.

1. You will pay a lot of money. The expense can vary depending on the type of professional you hire, but expect to pay at least $1,000. The more complex your website architecture and the more pages and features like e-commerce and social media integrations, the more you will pay. Factor in the price of hosting, domain registration, graphic design, photography, stock imagery, and copywriting when estimating your expenses. (You may pay for these things if you do your website yourself, of course, but many people who green-light an estimate from a web developer fail to factor in these added expenses.)

2. They may not deliver your product on time. Stories are too numerous to mention about website development projects that failed to launch on time or website developers who simply stopped communicating, leaving

their clients in the dark about an accurate go-live date. When screening professionals, ask past clients about the launch phase for their project and whether it met their deadline and how communicative the developer was throughout the course of the project. Once you have settled on a developer, establish a regular check-in time, at least once a week, to review the progress and ask about the timeline. The clearer you are about your expectations, the more responsive your web professional will be.

3. You will have to decide who to hire. As I have indicated with my screening tips, you will have to do your due diligence when evaluating professional web developers and ultimately make a decision with which you are comfortable. This will be a task unto itself but is not to be taken lightly. You wouldn't let just anyone build your house. Your website is basically one of the places your business will live. Give it the attention and time it deserves.

4. Making significant changes midstream will cost you more money (and time). If you change your mind about significant (or even minor) architectural details or decide to add features not considered in the original estimate, you will pay more money. Anything that adds time or expense to the project will be absorbed by you, so if you know you have a tendency to change your mind, consider building the site yourself or at least realize that you will pay more for your indecision. If you do decide to hire someone, make sure you have planned out your site as thoroughly as possible before you request an estimate.

5. They may not share all of their knowledge with you. Not all web developers are as generous as others about sharing their expertise. If you know you would like to update your site yourself, tell the candidates you are screening and offer to pay extra for them to train you on how to add pages, rearrange the architecture, add images, and in general, make any changes you foresee making on a regular basis.

WordPress vs. Website Builders

Before you decide whether or not to build your own website, it can help to have a thorough understanding of website platforms. If you are planning to build your site from raw code, I am going to assume that you have the technical expertise to do so or are planning to hire a professional. If either is true, you can skip this section. If not, I attempt to give you an overview of the major technologies used to build websites separate and apart from coding a site from scratch.

WordPress

WordPress is what is called a **CMS**, or **customer management system**. It stands out from the crowd among CMS since it powers most of the internet and is far and away the most successful. There is really nothing you cannot do with WordPress, but you will need the technical expertise to set it up or hire someone to either train you on how to use it or build the site entirely.

WordPress is also unique in its ability to incorporate countless plug-ins that can give your website unlimited power in its ability to integrate social media and e-commerce platforms, serve as event registration tools, create stunning photo or video galleries, or change user interfaces. I also like the easy-to-use Yoast SEO plug in that WordPress supports, giving it significant advantage over website builders like Wix and Squarespace in its ability to optimize your website for Google searches.

You will most likely pay more on the front end for a WordPress website but will save money over time since you don't pay a monthly subscription fee. You pay a one-time price for the theme but will likely pay someone to develop the site. I have found WordPress developers willing to start a website for me, train me on how to add pages and images, and serve as a resource for adding other features like mobile responsiveness. (Mobile responsiveness is a fancy way of saying that your website will look good on phones and that it will respond on devices like smart phones and tablet computers.) This "hybrid" arrangement of hiring someone and DIY can be a great way to keep your costs down and create a final product you are truly proud of.

Another advantage to using WordPress is that you retain full control of your images. When you use website builders like Wix and Squarespace, migrating later to a WordPress site can be extremely time-consuming and frustrating.

Website Builders

Website Builders like **Wix** and **Squarespace** both give you the option to start building a website and offer drag-and-drop ease of use. Both are excellent, but I find Wix to be the most intuitive and the easiest to customize. Squarespace templates, however, are routinely ranked more favorably by users in design and range of choices. It used to be true that SEO was severely lacking among drop-and-drag website builders, but these platforms have made great strides to improve their search engine optimization. Wix offers an advantage over Squarespace with its Wix SEO Wiz feature that helps users set up their SEO with appropriate keywords. Squarespace offers SEO tools too, but they are not as interactive and instructive as Wix.

Both Wix and Squarespace provide a wizard tool to help you start your website and begin editing it within mere minutes. Again, I like the Wix wizard tool better, which it calls ADI. It gives you choices along the way such as the type of business, the design palette, and the features you plan to incorporate and then creates a website that is, in most cases, truly impressive in its aesthetic appeal and customizability.

As for pricing, Wix and Squarespace are comparable, and both include hosting and a range of pricing tiers. The lower-priced tiers on Squarespace offer you more features, but Wix offers a larger range of tiers, making it more affordable over the long haul. Website builders also make it easy to convert your site for viewing on mobile devices like smart phones and tablet computers.

Before you decide to hire a professional, I invite you to create a website with Wix or Squarespace. With Wix, you will not have to spend any money until you tie it to a domain, and you will have a chance to see if you enjoy the process of building a site. (Squarespace doesn't offer a free plan but does offer a fourteen-day trial.) If building a website yourself proves too frustrating, you will then know that you should hire a professional. If, however, you enjoy the process, you will reap the benefits of total control over your website and pick up a new highly marketable skill.

Website-Building Checklists

Whether you have decided to take on the challenge of building your website yourself or hiring a professional website developer, you will still need to put certain things in place to ensure as smooth a process as possible. The first checklist—**Website Development Master Checklist**—is meant to cover all the steps of building your website. The second checklist—**DIY Checklist**—covers all of the steps you will want to cover as you get ready to build your own site. The third checklist—**Hiring a Pro Checklist**—prepares you for working with a website development professional.

Even if you are clear about wanting to build your website yourself, I encourage you to work through all three checklists since you will want to have a professional you can turn to for assistance if you find yourself outside your depth. These professionals can save you vast amounts of time, so I urge you not to dismiss this tip. If you are patient, you can find a professional who will offer as much or as little assistance as you need. Just be clear about expectations and take care not to waste their time by soliciting free advice. Always pay them for their time and generously express your appreciation.

Website Development Master Checklist

Whether you hire someone or not, this checklist will put you in the right frame of mind and arm you with the knowledge and confidence to create a website you can proudly claim.

☐ **Choose the platform with which you will build your website**. This factor will affect all of the other decisions here, so it needs to come first. If you are opting for raw-coding of your website (coding your website from scratch instead of using a website builder or WordPress), this checklist will still serve you.

☐ **Find a hosting company that is highly recommended**. I have had good luck with Bluehost, but I understand if you want to support a local company. Pick one that can support the platform you choose and offers reliable tech support that has tech support personnel with whom you can communicate easily and access 24/7. Always make sure your website isn't locked to any one host so you can migrate your site, if necessary. When comparing rates, pay attention to what they charge to add customer emails and to add bandwidth.

Read the reviews of host companies you are considering and try calling a customer service representative to vet their client care skills. Ask them:

- *How hard is it to migrate my site if necessary?*
- *Would you be willing to talk me through my hosting dashboard once I set up an account?*
- *What are your tech support hours?*
- *What is the process involved with resolving a tech support issue? (Do you have to email first and then wait for a call?)*
- *Where do their tech support representatives reside (i.e., in the same time zone as you)?*

☐ **Reserve your website domain**. Personally, I think it is convenient when the same company you hire as a host can reserve your domain. Bluehost offers this option, but not all hosting companies do. If this isn't important to you, that's okay, but it will give you more passwords and accounts to track. Keep careful records of all of your accounts and passwords, keeping them in both a file on your hard drive and a physical file folder.

☐ **Hire a graphic designer to create your branding**. While branding goes far beyond your logo, business name, tagline, and typeface, these four elements are the four columns of your brand. Your brand represents everything you do, so take the time to invest in a consistent look and feel. Your brand should reflect your values, so start there. Like your values, a brand you can be proud of will guide every decision you make in your business, so invest the time and expense it takes to create one that you can proudly claim.

☐ **Decide what kinds of images you will use**. You may be planning to create a website with illustrations, photography, or a mix of the two, but make some decisions early on about where you will source your images. If you are planning a photo-heavy site, Wix and Squarespace will provide an impressive photo inventory, but if you are raw-coding or using WordPress, you will need to find images in places that offer free photography like Unsplash.com or paid stock imagery sites like GettyImages.com or iStockPhoto.com. (Most paid stock imagery sites also offer illustrations.) You can always, of course, hire illustrators and photographers, who would happily welcome the work and give your website a decidedly distinctive edge.

☐ **Choose an image editor**. Image editors allow you to crop, rotate, resize, and reformat images. The most powerful one is Photoshop, but it is difficult to use and expensive. A free editor like Pixlr.com or BeFunky.com should serve your needs. Consider using Canva.com to create graphics, if you have some comfort or familiarity with graphic design. It is free (or low-cost, if you decide to invest in paid images and illustrations) and can help you create truly stunning imagery for surprisingly little time (once you spend a little time to thoroughly learn its tool).

☐ **If you plan to share audio or video files, choose the appropriate audio and video players**. These files are notorious storage hogs, so try to find players that let you store your files elsewhere. If you plan to create a lot of video content for your site, invest in an account with YouTube, Vimeo, or Wistia and then embed your website with the code so that viewers stay on your website, but the video isn't taking up space on your host server. WordPress offers some excellent media plug-ins like WordPress Audio Player that allow you to embed audio without sacrificing bandwidth, and SoundCloud gives websites on any platform the option to embed and play audio while storing the files on SoundCloud.

☐ **Research website e-commerce tools carefully if you plan to sell anything**. The right website development professional can help you make this decision but make certain they have experience building e-commerce sites. This feature complicates website development, and you want to make sure this piece is implemented correctly to ensure secure financial transactions and a smooth shopping experience for your customers. If this is your first website and online retail will be a major revenue source for your business, hire a professional. Wix and Squarespace both offer online shopping features, and WordPress has several e-commerce plug-ins—WooCommerce being the clear favorite, with Shopify quickly gaining popularity too.

☐ **Decide what social media links to share on your site**. If you have Facebook, Instagram, Twitter, and Pinterest accounts (or any other social media platforms) linked to your business, decide which ones you want to use to promote your site and how and where you will list them on your site. Do you want people to share images or posts or just know that you have social media accounts with relevant icons that link to these accounts? WordPress has plug-ins that let you integrate feeds from major social media sites, which I only recommend if you consistently keep these sites updated.

☐ **Nail down your architecture**. Go back to **Step 4** to help you make a final determination about the number of pages your site will be and how they will be organized. Create an architecture map with paper and sticky notes and then transfer it to an online tool like PictoChart, CardSmith, or Trello. Keep a hard copy ever-present to refer to as you work.

☐ **Create a binder**. Remember on page 41 when I suggested creating a binder if you were "less a digital thinker" to track your pages and content? If you haven't already done that, I want you to do it now. Even in this digital age, a hard copy of your content will help you more quickly organize and synthesize your content and track your progress as you create your website. Create a tab for each high-level button and plastic sheet protectors to collect magazine pictures. Place your architecture map at the front of the binder. Include a tab that stores technical information like domain registration, hosting details, and passwords. (If recording your passwords makes you nervous in case your binder falls into untrustworthy hands, use a password protection app like Dashlane or RoboForm.)

DIY Checklist

If you have decided to take up the challenge of building your own website and have checked all of the boxes in the **Website Development Master Checklist**, take a moment to congratulate yourself. This task is not for the faint of heart, and your determination shows real courage. Before you begin, put these things in order to ease the process and provide yourself peace of mind.

If you have decided to hire a professional, take the time to read through this checklist and then work yourself through the **Hiring a Professional Checklist**. The **DIY Checklist** will familiarize you with the main steps so that you can more effectively manage the process.

☐ **Find a time and a place to work.** Even if you plan to frequent coffee shops as you build your website, make sure you have a place to work in  your office or home that is clearly dedicated to your web development project—a desk or table that no one else will pile their crap on or interrupt you every five minutes. Try to block out generous chunks of time every day to make progress so that you will feel like you are nearing the finish line. Even a day can break your momentum, so try to find time every day.

☐ **Create a timeline and stick to it**. Share it with an accountability partner or colleague to make sure you have external pressure to meet your deadline. Place your timeline on a wall where you will see it every day and it can exact its full measure of guilt.

☐ **Reach out early to find proofreaders and beta testers**. Ask friends and colleagues now if they will help you test your site once it nears the launch phase. Proofreading and beta-testing are not the same things, but there is overlap. Proofreaders should have excellent grammar and spelling chops, but they may also find and report broken links. Beta testers are focused on reporting the experience of using your site but may also find typos and grammatical issues. After your website has been thoroughly proofed by a professional proofreader, you are then ready for the beta-testing phase.

☐ **Hire a professional website developer for backup**. Interview and hire a professional to rely on in case you get in over your head. Use my hiring checklist to help you make the right choice, modifying it for your needs.

☐ **Start building your website**. Commit to a set time and place each day. Keep your binder with you at all times. Before you hire a proofreader and put your beta testers to work, review the **Website Development Master Checklist** starting on page 51 to ensure your website ticks all boxes.

☐ **Hire a proofreader**. Secure quotes from proofreaders for the overall job and commit to a specific timeline. Your website isn't live yet, so give your proofreader access by sharing your username and password. Alert beta testers of when you can expect proofreading to be finished and their work to begin.

☐ **Give your beta tester the green light**. Offer to pay beta testers twenty-five cents to one dollar for each typo or broken link to secure their thorough and avid engagement with the process. Give them access via username and password. Ask them to report on the logic of navigation—does it make sense? Did they find what they were looking for? Were all of their questions answered? If not, do they have ideas for how to clear up their confusion? Thank them with gift certificates.

☐ **Link your domain to your website** (and your host, if you haven't already done so). Keep careful track of the information related to your hosting and domain for the duration of your website's existence. Guard it as carefully as your children's birth certificates. You will need to refer to it again, and you will need to renew your domain every year or so. Neglecting this housekeeping point can cause your site to literally disappear and, worst case scenario, possibly result in the permanent loss of your domain.

☐ **Launch your website**.  Once you are confident that your website is error-free and as user-friendly as possible, you are in good shape to go live. You may be asking yourself, *What about Google and Google Analytics?* In **Step 7: Care and Feeding (AKA Maintenance)**, I review the steps of setting up your Google business page. This is a critical step, facilitating your ability to be found on search engines and procure Google reviews but is a project unto itself. It is not outside your depth, however. Since it relates to SEO and dovetails with long-term maintenance, I have chosen to address it in the last step of the workbook. Once your site is fully launched, proceed to **Step 7**.

Hiring a Professional Checklist

This checklist only has a few steps but each is absolutely critical. Do your due diligence when hiring a website professional, making certain the person is someone with whom you can truly communicate and trust to follow through with the work on time for a reasonable price.

☐ **Let your network know that you are seeking a website development professional.** Tell people you trust that you would appreciate their recommendations of reliable website development professionals who are 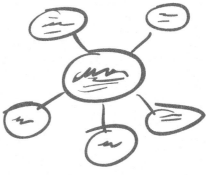 well-versed in the platform you have chosen. Once you have secured half a dozen or so names, start to review their portfolios and procure estimates. Make sure you know these things before you ask for a quote (and make these details clear to the professional):

- Your timeline
- The number of pages you expect your website to have
- Your overall architecture
- The status of the website's written content/copy (and whether you plan to hire a web copywriter either through the website professional or independently or if you are content with the existing copy)
- Your hosting company
- Your domain
- The features you expect your site to have (video/audio files, a blog, contact forms, downloadable PDFs, estimate forms, a shopping cart, etc.)
- Your requirements for meeting or checking in with the professional (and/or receiving updates about delays)
- Your expectations related to being trained to update the website

☐ **Interview professionals.** Once you have secured at least three estimates that you are pleased with, schedule interviews and ask about the following:

- Their experience with websites in your field
- Their expertise with websites with your features (particularly if your website has shopping cart and e-commerce features)
- Their plans related to proofreading websites (and access to professionals)
- Their beta-testing strategies
- Their security strategies
- Their correspondence habits (how they keep clients up-to-date about progress or technical issues)
- Their launch checklist
- Their experience with listing your website with Google and setting up Google Analytics
- Their SEO knowledge and track record (or access to SEO consultants)

If the estimates you receive far exceed your expectations, see if you can talk the price down. Be prepared to provide ready-made copy and graphics and oversee the proofreading, beta-testing, or launch phases (or all three).

☐ **Hire a professional.** I always recommend that you secure a contract with your website professional to ensure that your website content is fully under your legal control. Once the details are put to rest and your professional has agreed to a timeline, secure a set time each week—twice a week if you are eager to see the project completed—to check in and review their progress. Respond as quickly as possible to their requests to avoid delaying the project unnecessarily.

Assuming your professional will direct the proofreading and beta-testing phases of your site, you can content yourself with regular check-ins about your website and trust your professional to make steady progress and direct your website launch. Inform the professional that you would like to look through the website and work yourself

through the checklists starting on page 51 before you commence the proofing and beta-testing phases. Once your site is fully launched, proceed to **Step 7: Care and Feeding (AKA Maintenance)**.

Website Building Notes:

Use the space below to jot down notes about your website construction process. If you're still deciding on whether or not to build your website yourself, make your own list of PROs and CONs. If you have made a clear decision, use this space to jot down a timeline for getting started.

Step Seven
Care and Feeding
(AKA Maintenance)

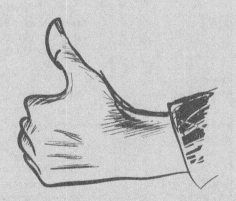

Congratulations! You have a website. In this step, you will put in place the main components to ensure that your site stays secure and up-to-date. You will also lay a foundation for getting your site discovered by Google and other search engines, so you don't feel like you're shouting into the void.

I have laid this section as a checklist, but since this is the most technical part of the workbook, I encourage you to read through it first thoroughly before you start actually executing the steps. This review process will give you a chance to familiarize yourself with the steps and ensure that you're not redoing tasks.

If you have hired a professional, ask them what parts of this process they are willing to help you execute, if you would rather take it off your plate. Be certain you know what steps have been executed and schedule a monthly check-in day to make certain everything is up-to-date and working properly (or hire someone to do so). I like to do it the first of every month. Put it in your calendar and reserve the time and an interruption-free quiet space to attend to it.

If your lizard brain is freaking out right now, screaming, "I can't do technical stuff! This is too much! No one told me I'd have to do this!" just remember to relax and breeeeeathe. I'm going to walk you through this, and it's really not that difficult. There will be times, however, in which I will direct you to online resources since Wix, WordPress, Squarespace and other website builders all vary in the way certain steps are executed.

Google My Business (GMB) Checklist

GMB is a free tool that gives you control over how your business appears on Google Search and Maps. Besides listing your business name, location, and hours, you can monitor and reply to customer reviews, add photos and videos, write blog posts, and monitor how people are searching for you.

Besides being a critical piece of the SEO puzzle, GMB is a great place to help your business get found and distinguished from competitors.

☐ **Log in to the Google account associated with your business (or start one).**

☐ **Go to Google.com/business and click "Manage Now."**

☐ **Enter your business name**.

☐ **Enter your business address**.
If appropriate, click the "I deliver goods and services to my customers" box. If you work from home or another address you don't want publicly displayed, click "Hide my address (it's not a store)." Then, click your "Delivery Area."

☐ **Choose your business category as accurately as possible.**

☐ **Add your business phone number or website**.

56

☐ **Choose a verification option**. You will be able to choose from several options to verify your business—postcard, phone, email, instant verification, or bulk verification. (I recommend instant verification.) Follow the prompts for the type of verification you choose.

☐ **Optimize your GMB listing**.

☐ **Enter your business name**.

Google (Bing and Yahoo) Submission Checklist

☐ **List your website in Google, Bing, Yahoo, and other search engines.**
A critical component of SEO is to establish visibility among popular search engines, with Google, of course, being the Goliath of the bunch. To be found on Google, Bing, or Yahoo, your website needs to be listed in their index. Follow these next steps to register your URL with the individual search engines.

☐ **Register your website with Google.**
Roughly two-thirds of all web searches are made through Google, which has evolved into the central interface of the entire internet. Even if you consider your enterprise low-tech, a presence on Google is paramount. To be clear, your website will only be found on Google if it is listed in Google's index. Below are the steps to do so:

☐ **Create a Google account.**
To submit your URL to Google, log on to Google's start page and create an account (free of charge). Click the "sign in" button and then select "create account." Google will then take you through the registration process.

☐ **Start Google Search Console.**
You can find the Google Search Console at search.google.com/search-console. (You will need to log in there before proceeding to the dashboard.)

☐ **Submit your website to Google.**
In the Google Search Console, you can register your website in the left sidebar. Click on the "add property" button, and a cursor appears at the same position. As already explained, enter the entire URL of your domain or webpage there. Then click on the "+ add property" button to submit your indexing request.

☐ **Verify your website.**
Google uses "spiders" to crawl through your domain regularly once you have registered, but a sitemap informs the crawling system about new web pages and provides data that helps crawlers react more quickly to changes and errors. (This is just one reason it is imperative that you keep your website up-to-date, besides being a generally good business practice. More on this later.)

Once you have registered your site as described, you can "verify" your website with Google Search Console. Since this process will vary depending on the way your website was constructed, I advise you to Google "verify my website with Google" and "Wix," "WordPress," "Squarespace," "[insert website builder]"—whatever you used.

Wix and Squarespace have excellent resources to direct you through this process, and there are myriad sites with instructions on how to verify your website with WordPress. Your hosting company should also be able to help you through this process. (This is another reason a hosting company with excellent customer service is worth paying a little extra for.)

☐ **Another Option: Manually Index Your Site with Google.**
During registration with the Google Search Console, Google states that your submitted URL will not automatically be accepted into the search index. Website addresses transferred to Google are first crawled by search bots within a few days and checked for relevance. Once your website has been set up according to Google's Guidelines for Webmasters, you should be well on your way toward successful registration.

The **Google Search Console o**ffers excellent resources on this topic. Go to **support.google.com** and type in "verify my website" to find a link called "Verify your site ownership" that leads to a page offering prompts and instructions on how to complete this process. If this feels like technical overload, consult a web development professional.

SEOSiteCheckup.com offers a great tool at **https://seositecheckup.com/tools/sitemap-test** to help you see if your website has a **sitemap.**

☐ **Set up a Google Analytics Page.**
There is no better reason for setting up your page on Google than **Google Analytics**. It is an invaluable resource for:
- Tracking and understanding your website viewers
- Seeing how they behave on your site
- Predicting the content they might want to see on your site
- Measuring your website's traffic goals
- Verifying the ROI of your web and social media presence

The good news? It's free. The not-so-good news? It can be challenging to set up. I recommend you hire a professional, but if you want to tackle it yourself, Hootsuite.com and Google.com both have excellent blow-by-blow articles that are easy to follow and offer visual references to walk you through every step.

There are several pieces of data you can get from **Google Analytics**:

- Your website's overall traffic
- The websites your traffic came from
- Individual page traffic
- Amount of leads converted
- The websites your leads came from
- Demographic information of visitors (e.g. where they live)
- Whether your traffic comes from mobile or desktop.

☐ **Register your website with Bing and Yahoo.**
Even though Bing and Yahoo are now powered by the same source and are tiny fish in the big internet pond, listing your website with these search engines is worthwhile. They are both gaining ground quickly, and it can never hurt you to be more visible.

☐ **Create a Microsoft account.**
Navigate to Bing.com and sign up for a free Microsoft account. Click on the "Sign in" button in the upper-right corner of the screen and then click on "Microsoft account." Enter the information required.

☐ **Set up Bing Webmaster Tools.**
Once you have registered your account, you will have access to several Bing Webmaster Tools. Like Google, Bing users are also prompted to enter their URL when indexing and then required to verify themselves as the owners.

☐ **Enter your website and sitemap.**
You can forward your sitemap to Bing and Yahoo by clicking on "configure my site." Generally, it takes a few days for your website to be indexed by the search engine. You can check the status of your application at any time.

Click on the button "Add website" to open a form. Configure the search settings and warnings via information about your website.

To do so, enter the complete URL of the sitemap in the "Add Sitemap" field. Usually it only takes a few days until your website is indexed by the search engine. You can check the current status using the status messages.

Website Security Checklist

Nothing sucks more than having your website hacked or compromised. You can lose your website data entirely or, at a minimum, be faced with paying a website professional several hundred dollars to recover your website. If you are storing clients' data, you will put others' privacy and financial information in peril and severely risk your professional reputation.

Take the time to put the infrastructure in place to keep your site as secure and safe as you would a brick-and-mortar location. Tend to it each month—bots are constantly on the prowl to detect vulnerabilities.

☐ Update your site regularly.

As soon as a new version of WordPress (or other CMS that you are using) is available, update it as soon as possible. WordPress users can sign up for a WP Updates Notifier to alert you to new releases. Remember that plug-ins may also need to be updated from time to time as well. Website builders like Wix and Squarespace will keep your site up-to-date and secure your site with an SSL certificate (more on this to follow).

For CMS users (like WordPress) and raw-coded sites, Securi.net offers an excellent tool called Website Application Firewall (WAF) that will provide added protection from hackers and other external threats.

☐ Keep your passwords secure and keep administrators to a minimum.

Protect your passwords as much as possible. Be prudent about the people with whom you share them and do not reuse them. Use random combinations of capitalized words, numbers, and symbols that are at least twelve characters and use passwords that are different from other accounts. Invest in a tool like Dashlane or RoboForm to store passwords securely.

Refrain from having any more administrators than necessary and shut down admin accounts when the people associated with them have finished their business relationship with you.

☐ Assign one website per server.

It can be tempting to store more than one website on a single server, but this can cause cross-contamination that makes all of your sites more prone to attack. If one site gets infected, the others are at risk, and cleaning up the damage is exponentially more difficult.

☐ Back up your website regularly.

Hire a professional if this is beyond your technical expertise. This can be a lifesaver. Make sure your backup is stored on a separate server and is done automatically. (Backups are not necessary with a website builder.) If you want to bravely attempt to back up your own site, Carbonite.com is a great resource that offers backup services for a wide range of bandwidths.

☐ Install SSL

SSL stands for **secure sockets layer** and establishes an encrypted link between a server and a web browser. (Website builders automatically install an SSL for you.) To find out how to install SSL, visit Securi.net and click on "Resources" and then "Guides." You'll find a link that leads to an article called "How to Install an SSL Certificate" that provides a thorough overview of the process.

Website Postbuild Checklist

Nothing sucks more than having your website hacked or compromised. You can lose your website data entirely or, at a minimum, be faced with paying a website professional several hundred dollars to recover your website. If you are storing clients' data, you will put others' privacy and financial information in peril and severely risk your professional reputation.

Remember in **Step 1: Preplanning Your Website** when I asked you to review the **Website Prebuild Checklist**? The goal of that list at that time was to plant some seeds about your website and how it could reflect the best things about your business and help ensure that you were creating an optimal user experience for your clients.

Now that you have created your website, use this **Website Postbuild Checklist** to double-check that you are answering all of the potential questions your customers might have when they find you online. This time I left space with each checkbox item to jot down notes and put the specific step in parentheses that you might want to review if you can't yet check that box.

Does Your Website...

☐ Have a Focused Mission?

Does your website project a clear mission and focus? Is its messaging clear and consistent? *(Step 1)*

☐ Convert Viewers Into Clients and/or Followers?

Is it converting users into customers by leading them to the landing pages? If they are navigating to landing pages, are they purchasing a product, booking an appointment, or signing up for an event or class? *(Step 1)*

☐ Invite Active Engagement?

Does it invite users to return or to try, buy, or subscribe? Does it stimulate their curiosity or inform or surprise them? Does it leave an impression? How do graphics, illustrations, and photos attract interaction? Does it leave them wanting more? Why should they return? *(Step 2)*

☐ Offer Clear Navigation and a Fluid User Experience?

Is its navigation logical and intuitive? Does it offer different brains alternative ways to make their way toward landing pages? Are buttons and links easy to read and understand? Can people easily trace their way back and easily return to pages they may be looking for? *(Step 4)*

☐ Offer Easy-To-Find Contact Information?

Is the contact information easy to find? I like to see contact information on every page. *(Steps 4 and 5)*

☐ Brand You Well?

Is your website consistent with your brand? Is the branding consistent with the messaging and graphics throughout the site? (We'll talk more about branding in **Step 2: Understanding Your Audience**.) *(Steps 1, 2 and 3)*

☐ Look and Feel Consistent Throughout?

Does the site feel, sound, and look consistent throughout its pages? Is it written in the same tone and from the same perspective (third person or first person, for example)? Does the imagery look like they are cohesive and harmonious? *(Steps 2 and 3)*

☐ Have a Platform That Is Easy to Update?

Is your website developer willing to show you how to update your site? Are you willing to learn? If neither of these is true, are you willing to pay someone to update it every time you want to make a change? *(Step 6)*

☐ Save You Money by Generating Sales with a Minimum of Effort?

You're a busy entrepreneur and need to spend your time working on various aspects of your business. Your website takes care and feeding but should not be a complete time suck. It may take time, but if you invest the time it takes in your site navigation and your SEO, your website should generate sales on its own, if you consider that a worthwhile goal. *(Step 5)*

☐ Attract Referral Partners?

Does it attract professionals who will likely refer business to you? Does your website or blog offer information and insight that engages your referral partners? *(Step 5)*

☐ Reach Markets You Want to Reach, Not Limiting You to a Geographic Area (If You Have Set Your Sights Beyond Your Local Area)?

If you are hoping to reach beyond your immediate area, does the website speak to this, or does it limit you geographically? If you are focused on a specific area, does it reflect the culture of that area? How so? *(Step 2)*

☐ Stay Under Your Control?

Are you in complete control of your hosting and domain, including all passwords? Are charges for both under your control? (They should always be; be conscientious about keeping that information current.) *(Step 1)*

☐ Feel Expensive to Create or Maintain?

If you have hired someone else to build it, are you certain there are no hidden expenses? Are they willing to train you on how to update and maintain it, both with content changes and technical updates? *(Step 6)*

☐ Appear Easily to the People Who Are Searching for You?

There's never a better time than when you're building your website to have SEO in mind. Chances are someone out there right now is looking for a business like yours, but she can't find you if your website isn't optimized for the search words she's using. *(Steps 4, 5 and 6)*

☐ **Create Excitement In Your Ideal Client When They Find You?**
You should be proud to refer your website to people and feel confident that its content and features are doing everything humanly possible to promote your business. Ideally, it will stir an emotional reaction in your prospective clients and make them feel like they *must* buy your product or service or they *can't wait* to meet you. *(Steps 2 and 3)*

☐ **Talk to Your Social Media?**
All of the social media accounts for your business should have icons representing the various platforms on every page of your website (in a static header or footer). Your blog posts should be set up to encourage shares and likes. *(Steps 2, 3 and 6)*

☐ **Feature Mixed Media?**
The more media—photography, video, downloadable files—the better. It's not only good for your SEO, it makes you look like you're truly engaged with your business and gives your client more reason to linger and interact. *(Step 2, 4, 6 and 7)*

☐ **Prize Quality Over Quantity – Attract The "Right" People, Not Just The "Right Number" Of People?**
You may attract millions of viewers with your site, but if they're people who will never buy from you or engage with the site, does it matter? That tree fell in the forest, and no one heard it. Is your target audience finding you, and if so, are they spending time on the website, purchasing, or spreading the word about your site with excitement and vigor? *(Steps 2 and 3)*

☐ **Have An Elegant, Easy-To-Use Shopping Cart?**
If your website has e-commerce functionality, is it easy to navigate and understand? Does it offer appropriate options (shipping + handling) and make it clear when users can expect delivery of products or services? Will they see an automatic confirmation response page after they click "Submit" or "Buy Now" and receive a follow-up email? Do you test this feature regularly? *(Step 4)*

☐ **Facilitate Optimal Customer Service (Return Policies, Answer Complaints, etc.)?**
Does your website answer all of the commonly asked questions with its FAQ section or offer easy-to-understand refund policies (or explicitly state that you don't offer refunds)? *(Steps 3, 4 and 5)*

☐ **Make It Easy To Connect With You (Quickly)?**
Does it invite further engagement and seem like a place where people want to spend time? Does it reflect the personality and values of your business? Does it feel like your "virtual boutique"? *(Steps 1, 2 and 3)*

☐ ***Not* Look Like A Graveyard?**
Does it look like it's lively and up-to-date? Are the events listed already passed? Are the blog posts recent? Does it have a dated, out-of-style look? *(Steps 2, 3 and 5)*

☐ **Have a Google Business Page and a Google Analytics Account that You Can Check Regularly?**
If you've hired someone to build your site, are they setting up the Google Analytics? Are they willing to show you how to use it or refer you to someone who will? (Expect to pay extra for this training.) *(Step 7)*

☐ **Is It Set Up To Receive Technical Maintenance From Time To Time?**
Is there someone more technical than you whom you can turn to for assistance when your get out of your depth? Have you built it into your calendar to do testing every month or quarter to test links, forms, and shopping features and ensure that appropriate tools are updated and working fluidly? *(Step 7)*

Spread the Word about Your Website

"Build it and they will come," a voice famously told Kevin Costner's character in *Field of Dreams*. And they did. But in your case, building the website means you're only halfway toward realizing the full potential of its ability to promote your business.

Once you have your website listed on Google and other search engines, start telling everyone you know or who would possibly be interested. Here are a few tips for attracting traffic to your website and encouraging people in your sphere to help share and endorse your web presence, both online and in real life.

1. Email Your Spheres

Let everyone in your personal and professional spheres know that your site is up and ready for business. Consider using a newsletter tool like MailChimp to create an actual newsletter that includes links to various parts of your website. You could present it in a personal-note format with little to no pictures to invite them to check out your website or use graphics and pictures to invite a more visceral, visual experience. Trust your gut in choosing the right approach—the more visual and creative your business, the more likely a graphics-laden newsletter is the right approach.

If you are skilled in using a **CRM**, you could create a mass letter that looks like a personal note but is written to several different segments of your sphere or audience with tags. For instance, you could use tags like "clients," "referral partners," and "friends" to delineate each group and write a separate letter template for each tagged segment. They will not necessarily know that you are sending the letter en masse and may be more likely to respond readily to your request and forward the news to people they know who may be interested. Use this approach judiciously and write a letter for each segment that conveys warmth and appreciation for their time. Respond immediately if they write back with congratulations and offers to help spread the word.

2. Use Facebook and Other Social Media

Start by creating a social media plan to provide clarity for yourself about your social media presence and set goals with measurable objectives and a cohesive strategy. Research articles online for guidance in creating a social media plan and stick with the social media platforms that you truly enjoy. If you hate LinkedIn, don't use it. If it's imperative that you use it, hire someone to represent your business who understands you and your brand.

If you are including a blog or have a podcast or video presence on YouTube, Facebook, or Instagram, use these media to announce your launch. Invite people to guest-blog or serve as interview subjects that you know have significant pull with your intended audience. Offer to be a guest on their blogs, podcasts, video blogs (vlogs), or Facebook Live broadcasts.

Consider buying social media ads on LinkedIn, Instagram, and/or Facebook. These ads are still super-cheap in comparison with other media, yet offer, in most cases, better analytics and tools for targeting people with specific demographics. Make a short video and share it with everyone who will listen in the social media world that you are excited to announce the premier of your new website and would love to invite them to check it out. Start with the compelling "why" that drives your business and include enough information to tease them to find out more but not so much that you irritate them or make them sleepy.

3. Plan a Launch Event (Virtually, In-Person, or Both)

Plan an actual party or online event (think a web-based virtual party or Facebook Live shout-out) and reward the first fifty viewers who try, buy, or subscribe with some special offer. Try to make it an actual item that you will send them—a product you sell, a bit of swag, a gift card, or a coupon. (Make sure you are set up to collect their mailing addresses if sending them something in the mail.)

If you take the tips above and write a blog, shoot a video, or record a podcast with social-media-savvy referral partners and influencers, ask them to share that media with an announcement of your new website with their audience and your special offer for the first set of visitors. (Offering to list their website as a link on your website somewhere, such as a resources page, and asking them to do the same for you is also great for your mutual SEO performances.)

4. Make Moo Cards.

If you are familiar with Moo printing services, found at moo.com, you know that you can make business cards and postcards through them that let you put up to one hundred different images on the back of the card. Brainstorm five to ten eye-catching slogans or questions to place in large fonts on the back. When you first launch your website, print up a stack of at least five hundred business cards or postcards and throw them down at places your target clients frequent and hand them out like candy.

To give you an example, a career coach could print some with these taglines, a different one for each card:

Quit your job. Find your career.
Revolutionize your work.
It's never too late to create your life's work.

Find work that matters.
Stop complaining and fix your career.

Don't be afraid to use humor to get attention. A tax accountant could print cards up with these taglines:

Your crumpled-up receipts are music to my ears.
April 15 shouldn't be scary. It's not Halloween.
Your taxes will not prepare themselves.
No one ever says, "Happy Tax Day!" Except me.
Keep more of what you earn.

A coworking space could target coffee shops where people tend to work who may be sick of the coffeehouse-with-laptops work scene:

Find your tribe.
Stop working in a coffee shop.
Surround yourself with inspiration.
Don't settle for working alone.
No one achieves great things on their own.

The front of the business card or postcard could feature the standard information and suggest the reader find out more about the business by checking out the prominently displayed website. You could even give each card up to one hundred different promo codes and set up your site to send them something special if they **try**, **buy**, or **subscribe**.

In Conclusion

Now is the time to heave a huge sigh of relief. You should be quite proud of yourself. You have created or managed the production of a website—something most people don't do and would never even attempt. As you know by now, your work is not done since websites are dynamic and require constant updating, but the lion's share of your website project is complete.

I don't think anything quite helps you deeply understand your business and its purpose like the creation of a website. You have really had to work hard to get in the head of your potential clients and understand how they might be scanning the horizon and settling on you as their target. If you keep communicating with your clients, tracking your analytics, and adapting and modernizing your content as needed to respond to their wants and needs, there will be no stopping you.

In closing, I offer a glossary as well as a list of resources for you to keep building your website and social media knowledge.

It is truly a brave new world, and the manner by which we all are consuming tangible and intangible products and services is changing dramatically every day. It can be daunting to feel like you need to keep up with new technologies and social media platforms. Don't feel like you have to know everything about every little online trend and fad but do keep your mind open to the seemingly strange or inexplicable.

In fact, it has never been a better time to invest long-term in your website and overall web and social media presence. In 2018 and 2019, online sales grew 15 percent

and show no sign of slowing down anytime soon. In 2018, e-commerce sales made up 10 percent of total US retail sales, totaling $126 billion for the 2018 holiday season.

Make time or hire someone to maintain and build your online presence, or your competitors will race by you like coked-up rabbits with their hair on fire. I recognize there's stark imagery in that metaphor, but I want to make certain this sentiment stays with you, even if I have to scare you a little bit.

Hopefully, this process has shown you that web development can and should be fun. You can show up authentically, express your entrepreneurial gift with creativity and flair, and truly connect with your clients as much or as little as you choose. Most of all, you can run your business on your terms and build a web presence and brand that leave a lasting impression and make you proud to hang your shingle.

Glossary
Common Web Development Terms

Glossary

Architecture: Refers to the way we structure a website to ensure a better experience for your visitors.

Call to Action: See **Landing Page**

Customized Email Addresses: An email address assigned to a specific domain address, such as kristin@sparkbusinesscoaching.com or even findoutmore@brightsidespace.com.

DNS (Domain Name System): System for converting alphabetic names into numeric **IP** addresses. When you type a web address (URL) into a browser, **DNS servers** return the IP address of the Web server associated with that name.

DNS Servers: See **DNS (Domain Name System)**

Domain: An actual presence on the Internet, such as a web page. Technically, a web domain name is a substitute that replaces the **Internet Protocol (IP) address**. We more commonly think of a domain name as as something like bipartisancafe.com. The purpose of a domain name is to help visitors locate your web site with minimal effort.

Header (h1) Tag: HTML tag that indicates a heading on a website. HTML has six different heading tags — h1, h2, etc. The h1 is considered the most important tag, and the h6 is the least important. See **Subhead Tags**

Host/Hosting Provider: A hosting provider provides a place on a web server to store all of your files and is responsible for delivering the files of your website as soon as a browser makes a request by typing in your domain name. BlueHost and GoDaddy are commonly known hosting providers. It's basically where your website lives.

Internet Protocol Address (IP Address): Unique string of numbers separated by periods that identifies each device using the Internet Protocol, defined as a number like 203.97.195.109, to communicate over a network.

Landing Page: A page on a website with a **call to action** that viewers are strategically led to through the navigation of the website or from a digital marketing campaign using social media platforms like Facebook and Instagram. A **call to action** asks website viewers to take an action like making a purchase, downloading a PDF, subscribing to a newsletter, thereby making a website a conversion tool.

Navigation: The process of navigating a network of information resources in the World Wide Web with a web browser, such as Google, Bing or Yahoo. The process of moving throughout the pages of a given website is also called navigation.

Primary Navigation/High-Level Navigation: The content that most users are interested in and are able to access from the Home page. Importance is relative; the type of content linked from the primary navigation on one website may be the same kind linked from the secondary navigation on another (for example, general information about the company or person).

Primary Users: The members of the target market that you are specifically hoping to attract.

Referral Partners: Professionals who will naturally refer business to you since your service often serves their clients' needs or helps them check some common task off their to-do list.

SEO (Search Engine Optimization): SEO is the use of keywords, strategies, techniques and tactics used to increase the amount of visitors/traffic to your website by obtaining a high-ranking placement in the search results page of a search engine like Google, Bing, and Yahoo.

SEO Keywords: The keywords and phrases in your web content that make it possible for people to find your site via search engines. A website that is well optimized for search engines "speaks the same language" as its potential visitor base with keywords for SEO that help connect searchers to your site.

SSL (Secure Socket Layer): Protocol developed for sending information securely over the internet. SSL establishes an encrypted link between a server and a web browser to keep all information private and protected.

Secondary Navigation/Lower-Level Navigation: The content that is of secondary interest to the user and is accessed at a lower level of the architecture than Primary Navigation pages. Any content that does not serve the primary goal of the website but that users might still want would go here. For many solopreneur websites, this might include links for "Rates" or "About Me."

Secondary Users: Individuals besides **primary users** who might use your website, such as referral partners, media, strategic partners, employees, newsletter subscribers, vendors, investors, influencers, reviewers, affiliates, etc.

Site Map A flow chart schematic that tracks of the organization of a website's pages. Ranging from simple to complex, site maps are the best way to communicate with a web developer or collaborator on how to build the site and how to manage its design as it grows.

Splash Page: A website with one page or just a few pages well-suited for projects with a specific focus and a limited amount of information. Business owners and event planners often use splash pages to announce the launch of a website, product, service, or event. A splash page is usually a **landing page** in and of itself.

Subhead (h2, h3, h4, h5, h6) Tags: Also called subheader tags, subheads help organize the importance of your website content in descending order from h2 from h6.

Touchpoints: See **UX (User Experience)**

URL (Uniform Resource Locator): The global address of documents and other resources on the World Wide Web. (Your URL is basically your website address but includes the "URL prefix," which are usually http:// or https://. The rest of the website address is the server name or IP address, like www.spark.com or even simply spark.com . The entire URL is https://www.sparkacareer.com.

UX (User Experience): Refers to a style of design that deeply considers how a person responds as she interacts with a product or tech tool. UX (sometimes called UI, for "user interface") references **touchpoints**, which are the various ways people will interact with your brand before they are ready to act. These can include visual displays, online ads, word of mouth, print marketing materials—anything that leads people to your business.

Made in the USA
Coppell, TX
07 November 2022